## *Additional Praise for*
## The Ensemble Practice

"*The Ensemble Practice* is the most practical 'how to' guide on building a thriving ensemble practice of anything available. Finally, a fulsome, step-by-step handbook on not only how to build one, but how to create the elements for it to thrive, including clear examples of pitfalls to avoid. Worth a read by new ensembles and those with $1 billion+ practices."
> —Valerie G. Brown, CEO, Cetera Financial Group

"Philip is one of the nation's most knowledgeable practice management consultants. In the *Ensemble Practice* he delivers an astounding compilation of practical information vital to any practitioner interested in growing his or her business. It's a must read."
> —Harold Evensky, President, Evensky & Katz

"In the financial advisory business, the phrase, 'eat what you kill,' has been the prevailing orthodoxy. Philip Palaveev, a long-time consultant to thousands of financial advisors, builds a strong case for cooperation and then 'sharing what you kill,' to push the metaphor. In short, Philip argues—convincingly in my opinion—that FAs should organize themselves in teams. Or, as he puts it, ensembles. There are many ways to do so, and many hurdles to overcome. In the end, the team-based service model can not only create efficiencies for the advisory practice but better serve its clients. (And that's the point right? Serving clients.) In this book, Palaveev show FAs—no matter where they work—how to go about doing it."
> —David A. Geracioti, Editor-in-Chief of REP. (formerly known as Registered Rep. magazine) and WealthManagement.com.

"Palaveev knows the wealth management marketplace better than anyone else and captured those industry insights that lead to creating a superior advisory firm."
> —Timothy D. Welsh, CFP, President, Nexus Strategy, LLC

# THE ENSEMBLE PRACTICE

Since 1996, Bloomberg Press has published books for financial professionals on investing, economics, and policy affecting investors. Titles are written by leading practitioners and authorities, and have been translated into more than 20 languages.

The Bloomberg Financial Series provides both core reference knowledge and actionable information for financial professionals. The books are written by experts familiar with the work flows, challenges, and demands of investment professionals who trade the markets, manage money, and analyze investments in their capacity of growing and protecting wealth, hedging risk, and generating revenue.

For a list of available titles, please visit our website at www.wiley.com/go/bloombergpress.

# THE ENSEMBLE PRACTICE

A Team-Based Approach to Building
a Superior Wealth Management Firm

**Philip Palaveev**

BLOOMBERG PRESS
An Imprint of
WILEY

Published by John Wiley & Sons, Inc., Hoboken, New Jersey.
Published simultaneously in Canada.

For general information on our other products and services or for technical support, please contact our Customer Care Department within the United States at (800) 762-2974, outside the United States at (317) 572-3993 or fax (317) 572-4002.

Wiley also publishes its books in a variety of electronic formats. Some content that appears in print may not be available in electronic books. For more information about Wiley products, visit our website at www.wiley.com.

*Library of Congress Cataloging-in-Publication Data:*

Palaveev, Philip, 1973-
    The ensemble practice : a team-based approach to building a superior wealth management firm / Philip Palaveev.
      p. cm. — (Bloomberg financial series)
    Includes bibliographical references and index.
    ISBN 978-1-118-20954-7 (cloth); ISBN 978-1-118-22869-2 (ebk);
    ISBN 978-1-118-26599-4 (ebk); ISBN 978-1-118-23138-8 (ebk)
      1. Financial planners.   2. Investment advisors.   3. Financial services industry.   4. Partnership   I. Title
HG179.5.P353 2013
332.6068—dc23

2012017196

Printed in the United States of America

SKY10069492_031224

*To Emilia, Kiril, and Stella—I love you!*

# Contents

# PART II: MANAGING AN ENSEMBLE

# Introduction

"No one can help you as much and make you as successful as your partners can," Ed Drosdick told me. Ed was one of my mentors and a longtime partner in Moss Adams, the firm where I started my career and where I worked for nine years. "Of course, no one can hurt you as much and make you as miserable as your partners can," added Ed. Both parts of this statement proved to be true in my own experience, and I am sure most professionals who have been in a partnership will easily agree. If I ever achieved any success, much of that I have to thank my partners for. If I ever stayed awake at night, grinding my teeth, my partners deserved the credit for that too.

This is a book about partnerships—how to start them, how to manage them, how to maintain them, and how to protect them. There is no point in talking much about how to break them—that part is easy. Most of the challenges presented to those who are trying to form or improve a partnership are hard ones—a complex mix of emotions, finances, and management structures. This book won't make the problems easier or offer immediate solutions, but it should give you many ways of analyzing the situation, many methods that have worked for other firms, and perhaps many suggestions for what not to do.

I have very little if any scientific basis for most of the recommendations in this book. You won't read many statements that are based on a random survey of 1,000 partnerships or a controlled lab experiment involving 30 managing partners (half of whom were given a real memo and half a fake placebo memo). The basis of this book is largely my experience consulting with over 500 financial advisory firms of various sizes. Much is also driven by my personal experience as an employee and then principal in Moss Adams and my tenure as president of Fusion Advisor Network. In other words, we will rely a lot on stories, case studies, and the scars that go with them.

The book is intended to be a comprehensive treatment of the subject with each chapter dealing with an important management issue or decision step. The chapters are written to be a self-contained discussion of the subject, and you are certainly welcome to read only selected chapters that deal with the decisions you are making. At the same time, there are a lot of interconnected issues that flow from one chapter to another, and my wish would be that you take the time to read the book the old-fashioned way—from cover to cover. I hope you enjoy it and find it helpful.

# Acknowledgments

My father was my first boss and my first teacher in business who taught me that a good business starts with pride in what you do and that integrity and ethics are needed the most when most people would find a reason to act differently. My father built a shipbuilding business from scratch in a country that was a couple of years removed from Communism, and he did it without ever succumbing to the corruption and circumstantial morals that mired the world around him. He always says, "No guts, no glory!" and he used his business to create a world of pride, honesty, and hard work and to teach those values to many. I don't think he even knows what he created. I think he is just focused on the next ship in the dock and wonders if he could have done more. Thank you, Dad!

I have to thank every single client I ever worked with as they let me walk into their business and examine and study what made them successful and what they struggled with. I have met so many amazing business people in the last 12 years that it is impossible to list them all, but I am thankful for each and every engagement. Fusion advisors are a special group of people—I have a hard time calling them clients. I feel the responsibility I feel to a client, but they are much more like friends. You have shared your business with me and I have learned so much from you.

I could not write so many pages about partnerships without my business partners over the years—Rebecca Pomering, Mark Tibergien, and Stuart Silverman. The three of you pretty much helped me "grow up." You have taught me so much; you have always treated me with such patience and care that I can never thank you enough.

Jonathan McQuade, my colleague in Fusion and my friend, completed all the research for this book and supplied the data analysis that went in the various charts and graphs. Jonathan is one of the rising stars in the investment business, and I look forward to all the interesting work ahead of us.

Last but not least, I need to thank my grandma, may she rest in peace, who provided most of the quotes and proverbs in this book. I remember hearing many of them directly from her, but now that I think of it, most of them came to me from my mother. I guess we learn the most from those that are closest to us.

# PART I

# Structuring an Ensemble

# CHAPTER 1

# The Ensemble Defined

"I like building a business; I just don't like managing people!" This oxymoronic phrase has defined the landscape of the financial advisory industry for decades as financial advisors have consistently focused on "hunting and gathering" new clients rather than the "unnatural" act of collaborating with other professionals. As a result, the majority of financial advisory practices today still function as "solos"—one man (or woman), alone against the markets and the tax code. This simple practice model unfortunately has always been fragile and inefficient, and it leaves no legacy behind when the advisor retires.

I believe there is a better model of practice—one that combines the skills and energy of multiple professionals and focuses on the cultivation of relationships with clients and employees to build a profitable and lasting structure. I know many advisors will agree with this statement since the multiprofessional practice we call *ensemble* is already being adopted and perfected by thousands of practices. The results are rewarding to the advisors who embark on building an ensemble and are changing our industry.

For the last 12 years I have had a chance to work with many financial advisory firms as a management consultant and observe their strategies, their plans, their culture, and their checkbooks. Many were following the traditional model of one-person-one-practice, but many were already building large and complex organizations. All of them were in some process of change and transformation—after all, the financial advisory industry is relatively new and quickly changing. What I found was that while the changes were purely quantitative for most solo practices (i.e., more revenue, more clients, but the same kind of practice), the multiprofessional ensembles I worked with were able to make qualitative changes that transformed them into better competitors and more valuable businesses.

I can't resist comparing the solo practice model with the hunter-gatherers of ancient times. Human beings have been roaming the earth for roughly 200,000 years. In the first 195,000 of years of their existence, however, they left very little trace of their activities,[1] their efforts, and their achievements. All that remains is a few arrowheads and doodles on cave walls—items of little interest to anyone outside the scientific community and which often prove to be pranks by drunken college students. It wasn't until several thousand years ago[2] that human beings started developing civilizations—complex societies that produced great cultural artifacts such as magnificent buildings, libraries full of books, scientific discoveries, and beautiful works of art. How is it that hundreds of thousands of years left so little trace but several centuries lead to such an explosion of knowledge and culture?

The answer lies in the discovery of agriculture and with it, the large, complex, and team-based societies that required carefully structured organization and provided enough resources to allow some of the members of those societies to focus on specialized tasks such as science, art, and religion. Once humans did not have to spend all of their time hunting or picking up fruits and berries, their creativity and inventiveness blossomed, and they started to write, to debate, and to pass knowledge and resources from one to another and from one generation to another.

In a similar way, the vast majority of financial professionals worked with their clients for decades and then retired with their practice dissipating behind them and the clients scattering to other advisors. The one-person practice has been the building block of the financial advisory industry for decades. That one person, the molecule of the profession, has always been a hunter-gatherer and has primarily been consumed with finding new clients. Since until the 1990s the business was mostly commission-based. "Hunting" (i.e., sales) was the primary activity and, just as it happened to our ancient predecessors, hunting left little time to write books or design pyramids. The best "hunters" dominated the brokerage "tribes" of the 1980s, and the quieter "engineer" types were poorly regarded, encouraged to learn to hunt, and often did not survive. To quote Michael Cera's character in the important movie *Year One*, who was in a prehistoric tribe, "We have two job descriptions here—hunters and gatherers—and you are obviously not good at hunting."

Fee-based financial advice was to the financial industry what agriculture was to our predecessors. As clients started to pay to have a percent of their assets managed for the ongoing advice of the professional,[3] suddenly there was a need for a completely new type of organization, new types of skills, and ultimately a new type of culture and values—"growing" became more important than hunting and "cultivating" more productive than gathering. Nurturing and preserving existing client relationships produces a reliable and predictable stream of revenues for the advisors and favors those that can retain clients rather than jumping from one client and transaction to the next. What is more, the fee-based advisory business created a surplus of time and resources, paving the way for the emergence of specialized responsibilities and a team-based, rather than individualistic, organizational structure.

This is very important to understand before we start building an ensemble—the recurring and predictable nature of the revenues allows an ensemble to exist. The more recurring and predictable the revenues are, the more the practice can have the patience to cultivate relationships and to train and develop staff. The more the practice has to constantly search for new revenues, the less likely it is to have this long-term focus and build an ensemble. If you don't believe me, try reading this book on an empty stomach and see how well you can focus on the page rather than the fridge.

## The Ensemble Concept

*The ensemble practice is a team of financial advisory professionals that relies on the team rather than an individual to service and manage client relationships.* The ensemble practice involves multiple professionals who often have specialized roles and bring different skills and knowledge. Ensembles also employ different levels of professionals, combining the enthusiasm, energy, and lower cost of less experienced advisors with the experience, wisdom, relationships, and network of highly experienced team principals—a process we will call *leverage*. Most of all, an ensemble is defined not only by its organizational structure but by its culture—a collective behavior that focuses on the team goal rather than individual agendas and says "we" more than it says "I."

As a result of leverage (multiple levels of professionals), specialization, the larger pool of combined resources, and the "two heads think better than one" effect, ensembles have performed better than other types of financial advisory practices. In fact, ensemble practices have proved to grow faster, attract larger client relationships, achieve higher levels of profitability, and create long-term value for their principals. What is more, they tend to survive the founding generation and pass their resources and knowledge to a new generation of professionals. Ensemble practices tend to create and invent more successfully—they develop new methods and ways of servicing clients and original analysis and planning processes. Last but perhaps most important is the fact that clients have shown a clear preference for working with ensemble practices and have overwhelmingly gone to firms that have been early adopters of the ensemble concept.

These are strong statements, and I will certainly try to substantiate each with statistical data, case studies, and examples from my experience as a consultant, starting with this chapter. As strong as the evidence in favor of ensembles may be, though, the majority of the advisory industry today still practices in individual solo practice with only one advisor responsible for business development (sales), service, research, operations, and everything else. Many firms, while consisting of multiple professionals, still perform like hunter-gatherers—that's why our criteria for an ensemble will focus on culture as much as we focus on the organizational structure. While the advantages of being an ensemble practice are accepted by most, the process of building such a practice is difficult, and the obstacles have led many advisors to prefer the control and path of less resistance of operating on their own. The industry today has more solo and silo practices (we will define them in a second) than ensembles.

Not all nonensemble practices are solo. There are many firms that have multiple professionals and even multiple partners but still do not practice a team-based service model. It is very common in the industry to see practices that have multiple principals but where each principal works with his or her own clients and to a substantial degree derives income from his or her own client base. We will call such firms *silos*. There is no clear way of differentiating a silo firm from an ensemble firm, but usually the most telling sign is the presence (or absence) of a shared bottom line that significantly impacts the income of the owners. In other words, if 40 percent or 50 percent of the income of a principal depends on the shared result of the practice, we are certainly working with an ensemble firm. If, on the other hand, the shared bottom line only determines 5 percent to 10 percent of the principal income while the personal results determine the remaining 90 percent to 95 percent, the firm is most likely better classified as a silo.

So to summarize, by their organizational characteristics (roles and responsibilities in the delivery of services to clients), here are the three types of practices we are discussing:

1. Ensembles—multiprofessional practices that deliver services as a team and pool all resources and profits.

2. Solos—individual practices with only one professional advisor. The solo practice usually has some support staff, that is, an administrative assistant or client services administrator, but does not have other professionals.
3. Silos—practices that have multiple professionals, but those professionals maintain their own clients and their own profits, in essence only sharing office space and a fax machine.

Note that ensembles do not necessarily describe the affiliation characteristics of the practice. How the practice is registered with regulators and how it works with its broker-dealer and other support resources (affiliation model) is not a critical factor, as we can find ensemble practices in every affiliation model.

## Ensemble Demographics

The practice of advisors working together in a team structure began to take hold in the late 1990s, particularly among independent financial advisors—those that own and operate their own practice as opposed to working as employees for a large firm. (The term "ensemble" itself was first used in 2001 in a research report published by Moss Adams LLP,[4] and I had the privilege to be part of the team that wrote that report.) There are reasons why independents developed and adopted the ensemble concept faster than the larger national firms, and the reasons have to do with culture and resources.

### Key Terminology

- Independents—firms that are majority owned and operated by the advisors who work in them. While by definition independents tend to be smaller, size is not the criterion—a large 30-partner firm is independent because the partners/owners are also the advisors, while a small bank-owned practice is not independent. The independents tend to practice in two primary affiliation models—registered investment advisors (RIAs) and independent broker-dealer affiliated advisors (IBD advisors).
- Large firms also known as wirehouses—big national firms such as Bank of America Merrill Lynch, Wells Fargo, Morgan Stanley Smith Barney, and UBS, where the advisors are employees of the firm rather than owners of their own practice. This employee model applies also to smaller firms where advisors work FOR the firm rather than on their own.

- Regional firms, insurance firms, and other types of firms—between affiliation models where the advisors are owners and models where advisors are clearly employees, there are many business models where the advisors have significant ownership of the practice but still are closely supervised and managed by a home office. This is true for many of the regional brokerage firms, the investment practices inside insurance firms, and even the branch offices of some of the independent broker-dealers. Again, the team-based ensemble model equally applies in this environment with some modifications for the areas of practice controlled by the home office.

We can try to explain why the independents have adopted the ensemble model more readily. The culture among the large investment firms in the late 1990s was still one of hunting. The firms encouraged and focused on production—that is, sales—and held in high regard those that produced the most (high producers). Production (sales) numbers were made public, rankings were released monthly, and there were many prizes and recognition associated with "hitting the numbers." Those that hit the number went on lavish trips and were given plaques to put on their desks, and those that missed the numbers were typically "coached" and treated as the main cabin on a trans-Atlantic flight (i.e., don't you dare use the first-class restrooms). This individualistic culture tended to favor and encourage big egos, and collaboration was simply not a value that was rewarded. In fact, I have met wirehouse advisors who would introduce themselves by their place in the production ranking—for example, "My name is John Scott. I am the third largest producer in our office." Branch manager compensation was based on production, so not surprisingly managers were not very likely to encourage the teaming of advisors even if the advisors themselves had an interest in doing that.

In contrast, advisors that were starting their own independent firm were often "refugees" from the producer cultures and resented the production-driven mentality. Many of the founders of independent firms left the larger firms precisely because of that sales culture. Many were actually encouraged to leave as they were not producing enough—turns out that they could not hunt deer but they could sure grow turnips.

The second factor for the emergence of ensembles among the independents was simply economic necessity, as startup independent firms had little resources and often needed to pool their limited capital and staff in order to achieve their goals. Many of the future partnerships started essentially as "roommates"—the advisors agreed to share an office and assistant because they could not afford to have their own. What started as sharing agreements often developed into a full-blown partnership; soon they were sharing clients, marketing, revenues, decisions, and ultimately sharing profits.

While the term *ensemble* was initially associated with independent firms, today it applies and is used in many large firms. Many advisors inside large national firms practice as a team with the same characteristics of team-based culture, specialization, and a multiprofessional service model. In fact, many large firms actively promote and encourage their professionals to form teams or join teams. While the producer culture certainly still creates resistance to such team structures, their results have been impressive and undeniable, and firms of every kind recognize them. In fact, even in the 1990s some of the large national firms were researching and experimenting with team-based service models. While for the most part the teams had trouble staying together and overcoming the natural friction that team formation brings, the experiments produced some of the early research and methodology that are still in use.

Today, an estimated 25 percent of all practices in the industry function as ensembles, as shown in Figure 1.1.[5] Ensemble practices continue to be much more prevalent among independent firms with an

**FIGURE 1.1** Percentage of Ensembles in the 2011 Registered Rep Compensation Survey

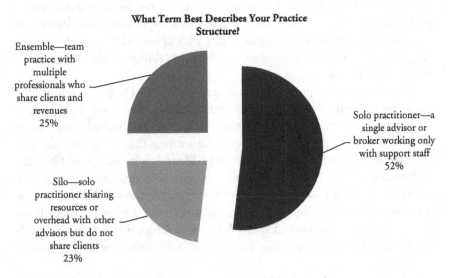

Source: "Registered Rep Compensation Survey 2011," Penton Media

estimated 35 percent of the firms having multiple professionals compared to 15 percent of employee advisors.[6] It is very difficult to test the culture of a team in a survey, and we stated that the true criterion for an ensemble is the use of "our" versus the use of "mine." Still, it is fair to say that the industry is changing and that the future belongs to the ensemble firms. They are attracting more clients than solo-focused firms, and most importantly they are attracting more new professionals—those that are just joining the industry—and they are doing a much better job of growing new talent.

## Ensembles Are More Profitable and Valuable

Needless to say, having more clients and revenues is not necessarily a goal in itself—the goal is usually the increase in profits. The simplest measure of profitability in an advisory firm is the pool of income available to the owners of the firm after all other expenses have been paid and capital needs have been met. That pool of income can be paid to the owners in the form of salaries, draws, or distributions, or simply be retained in the firm as capital. The decision of how to distribute the pretax income to partners is based on a combination of tax and compensation factors. For the purpose of discussing profitability, though, we will treat the entire pool available to the owners as a measure of how financially successful the firm is—the larger the pool, the more profitable the firm is. Of course, if a firm of five partners has a pool of pretax income of $1 million, it is by no means more successful than a solo practice with $500,000 in income. Thus we will consider the *pretax income per partner* as a balance measure of the profitability of the firm and its ownership structure.

Based on profits per owner as a measure, ensemble firms significantly outperform their solo peers (and most likely silos) (see Figure 1.2). A "mature" ensemble firm (meaning it is well established and not in transition) generates on average twice the income that a mature solo firm generates based on the results of the 2011 Moss Adams Survey of Financial Performance. That said, we note that mature solo practices actually earn nearly as much as early ensembles—that is, those making the transformation. We will discuss this need to invest in the practice and perhaps forgo some income in the next chapter. Super-ensembles, the largest ensemble firms, outperform mature solo practices by four times the pretax income per owner.

Profits, especially transferable profits, create equity value, and in the last 10 years, financial advisory firms have firmly established their equity value.

**FIGURE 1.2** Profit per Owner by Business Model

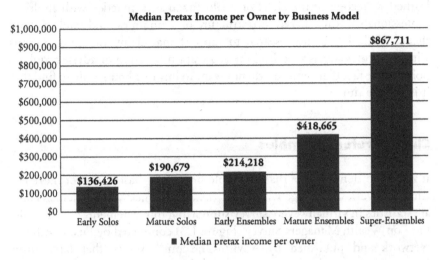

Source: 2011 Investment News/Moss Adams Adviser Compensation and Staffing Study

There is an active market for advisory practices with reliable and frequently published valuation information. Industry reports from such sources as FP Transitions (a Portland, OR, valuations and transaction support firm) and FA Insight (a Tacoma, WA–based market research firm) put valuations of advisory firms at an all-time high as of the time of writing this book. The number of transactions and the interest from buyers suggest strong liquidity and interest from buyers such as banks, CPA firms, other advisory firms, and consolidators.

All research reports unequivocally state that firms with multiple professionals are more valuable as measured by the price paid for a dollar of revenue. FP Transitions estimates that the presence of a second professional in the practice can increase the multiple paid for a practice.[7] A research report from FA Insight[8] states that the larger ensemble firms generate interest from the large and well-capitalized institutional buyers such as banks and consolidators while the small silo practices are restricted to smaller buyers with less capital, namely, other advisors. As a result, even if the valuation multiples between solo and ensemble practices do not show a dramatic differential, a deeper look may reveal that while ensembles are often acquired for cash and public company stock, solo practices have to wait for four to five years for a smaller and more risky buyer to make the payments.

It is also interesting to note that both small and large acquirers have learned to recognize the signs of a silo practice (a practice with multiple professionals but no shared infrastructure or economics) and tend to avoid them. While I have no research to support that claim, my conversations with the professionals who lead the acquisition function or advise acquirers point to the fact that acquirers do not want to buy one house only to find that it is really a duplex.[9]

## Clients Prefer Ensembles

It is easy to demonstrate that ensemble firms grow faster, attract more clients, and work on average with larger (i.e., higher net worth) clients. There are statistics in virtually every survey supporting this statement. For example, the Top Wealth Managers Survey (Figure 1.3) conducted by Fusion Advisor Network and published by AdvisorOne.com[10] shows that large firms (exclusively ensembles) have relationships that are seven to eight times larger than the smaller firms (mostly solo and silo firms). Still, that does not necessarily mean that clients prefer ensembles, that may simply mean that large ensemble firms are better marketers (they actually are).

**FIGURE 1.3** AUM per Client by Firm Size

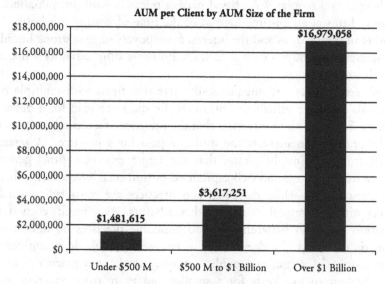

Source: "2011 Top Wealth Managers Survey" by AdvisorOne

Of the assertions I just made (more profitable, more valuable, and preferred by clients), this is the toughest one to back up. In fact, a U.K. survey done by Scorpio Research[11] actually found that clients prefer to work with one person backed by a small firm rather than with multiple professionals. In fact, intuitively most advisors understand the power of the one-on-one relationship and sometimes struggle believing that an ensemble can still have the same quality of relationships. Does this suggest that perhaps I was wrong and that it is more profitable for the business to involve multiple professionals in the relationship, but that clients would much rather "talk to the doctor directly" (no nurses and physician assistants)?

I personally believe that what clients value is the sense of trust, the sense that they are heard and understood, and that someone is responsible for everything that happens in the relationship. It is much easier to establish those three factors in a one-on-one relationship—after all, "trust me" is easier to develop than "trust us." The solo practice has a very easy time demonstrating that the advisor is listening attentively (no one else is in the room) and that there is a sense of responsibility ("it is just me"). That said, there is certainly a way to establish trust between a team and client and create the same atmosphere of communication and ownership. It will just require better coordination and a more carefully structured exchange of information. It will also require a culture of "everyone is responsible"[12] to alleviate clients' fear that the sense of "caring" will disappear.

Where ensembles shine and clearly have the advantage are two factors that are very important to clients but often overlooked by advisors—expertise and continuity. Where solo advisors often struggle is communicating their expertise in multiple areas to clients. After all, delivering wealth management services[13] requires knowledge of investments, financial planning, taxes, insurance, Social Security, and other laws and multiple other specialized topics. It is difficult to convey that one person knows all there is to know about all of those factors. On the other hand, this is where the specialization of a team is an advantage.

The second factor is "the bus question." Many of the solo advisors I have worked with have told me that clients ask, "Frank, what happens with our accounts and our plans if you get hit by a bus?" This may seem like a very unlikely (statistically speaking) possibility, but this is actually a deep concern of many clients. The concern is not just about the bus (bus drivers are among the most careful drivers you will encounter) but rather about the general possibility that the advisor may not be able to assist the client or may not be available. This includes vacations, illness, family emergencies, and everything else that may make one person unavailable. Relying on one person is such an unreliable strategy! As my friend and client Kathy Fish says, "A man is not a plan." The ability of ensembles to create that sense of continuity and reliability is a great advantage and much understood and appreciated by clients.

## Should Everyone Be an Ensemble?

Every practice desires to grow, and the reality of the financial advisory industry is that each professional can only work with somewhere between 40 clients (in a high net worth—focused wealth management firm) to 120 clients (in a more average practice with affluent clients). Once that limit is reached, there are only two ways in which professionals can grow their practice and therefore their income: (1) work more hours (most would rather not) or (2) increase the average size of a client relationship (difficult to do).

In my practice as a consultant in the industry, I have seen solo practices achieve amazing size. I have worked with some advisors who single-handedly manage as much as $1 billion in client assets. Those examples, though, are very rare. It is much more typical to see solo advisors hit that ceiling around $1.5 million in total revenues (approximately $150 million in client assets). At the same time, the largest ensemble firms in the industry today are headed for well over $25 million in revenue ($2.5 billion in client assets), and there are ensemble teams inside the national firms that manage as much as $12 billion in client assets.

While ensemble practices hold the promise of faster growth and better personal income for the principals of the team, I am very far from suggesting that every practice should try to become an ensemble. There are three primary reasons why an ensemble practice may not be the right fit for an advisor: the desire to have a higher level of control, preference for more a flexible lifestyle, and relatively small client relationships.

Control is a big factor in the sense of satisfaction and accomplishment that advisors get out of their practice. It is the reason why you are likely to meet many advisors with a small practice of their own who are much happier with what they have than the advisor with the largest practice in the Chicago office of a large national firm. The ability to influence your own environment, the ability to change what you don't like, and to leave your mark on anything from the software you use to the way you present financial plans to clients is critical to the sense of success an advisor gets from his or her practice. Unfortunately, when you are part of a team you surrender that control in exchange for the resources and support of the team. If you are insistent on not having to argue your decisions and explain your reasons every step of the way, if you want to be able to do what you feel is right 100 percent of the time, if you want to buy whatever you like without a committee meeting . . . well, an ensemble practice may not be for you since you will have to do all of those things—argue, explain, do things you disagree with, and sit through meetings.

Many practitioners also assign a high value to the balance of life they have—the ability to spend a lot of time with their family, to pursue their personal hobbies and interests, even to work only part-time. This also applies to the cost structure of the practice as such advisors prefer to keep low overhead and not experience the pressure of having to cover a larger bill and therefore maintain high overhead. Clearly, having multiple employees and having other colleagues results in more pressure to maintain a similar workload and contribution, as it is difficult to be lifestyle oriented in an ambitious team of people. Similarly, the costs of an ensemble practice are higher (more on that in Chapter 11) and require the practice to maintain a higher level of revenue.

Surprisingly, the final factor in the ability of a practice to become an ensemble is the size of its typical (target) client. It appears in my experience that there is a certain communication "overhead" that is incurred every time a team of people need to collaborate on a task or a project. Simply put, if an advisor is delegating portions of the client service to his or her team, that process of delegation and communicating what needs to be done will require some time. If, for example, servicing a client requires 20 hours of work in a year, chances are that one or two of those hours will be spent in communication and coordination between the team. This "overhead" of 5 percent to 10 percent (one or two hours out of 20) is pretty reasonable considering the efficiency of using multiple levels of professionals and specialists. Unfortunately, if the entire client service consists of four hours, spending an additional one or two hours communicating and coordinating will be prohibitive.

This is why practices working with smaller clients tend to have a harder time growing into an ensemble while firms that service very large relationships tend, almost by default, to favor a team structure. That's not to say that the team concept is impossible with small relationships, but it is more difficult to execute and requires a very efficient process of communications and service.

We just discussed the reasons why a practice may prefer not to be an ensemble from the perspective of the principals or owners. We should also discuss the reasons why an ensemble may not be an effective model from the client perspective. As we discussed above, clients have expressed strong preference for being surrounded by a team of practitioners. That said, clients value even higher the sense of relationship they have with the practice—if the client loses that sense of closeness, trust, and understanding, the relationship changes dramatically and not for the better.

It is very difficult in an ensemble to manage the line between team service and impersonal service, and ensembles are always in danger of crossing that line. If clients start feeling that they do not receive much attention from the senior members of the team and start feeling that they are being "delegated," that relationship will be in danger. If clients feel that they are surrounded by many professionals but none of them is really taking the lead in being the proactive driver of services, the relationship may once again suffer. We will discuss this in more depth in Chapter 7 but losing the personal connection with the client is perhaps the biggest danger for ensemble firms.

## What's Next and Who Should Read on

This is certainly a book that advocates the ensemble model and aspires to invite you to consider transforming your practice into an ensemble or perhaps fine-tuning the ensemble practice you already have. I hope by the time you turn the final page you are not only convinced that this is a good step for you as an advisor and business owner (the limitations mentioned above not withstanding), but also that you have a clear understanding of the steps in building an effective ensemble practice.

In the next chapters you will find a detailed roadmap to guiding your practice to a team-based service model. Not surprisingly, we will discuss organization and compensation a lot—after all, this is the strength of the ensemble, the ability to unite a group of people behind the practice. We will go through alternative ways of organizing service, compensating people, designing jobs and responsibilities, and structuring partnerships. Along the way we will consider the statistical data available and the research published in the advisory industry as well as in related industries. In fact, it is my belief that the transformation to ensemble practices in the advisory business follows the same process that is already complete in other professions. Just look around the next time you visit your doctor, your dentist, or your CPA. The same process is already complete and very much taken for granted in law firms, in public relations and advertising firms, and in architect firms.

You can find signs of the same business model in veterinary offices and perhaps even in fitness and personal training businesses and upscale hair salons (don't ask me how I know). The point is that the same process of specialization and leverage is universally applicable in most client services as long as the client relationship is large enough and the service is likely to be recurring.

Finally, the ensemble model of service and practice management should be applicable in financial advisory practices of every affiliation model. It should be equally applicable to registered investment advisors (RIAs) who actually use it the most, to advisors affiliated with independent broker-dealers (IBDs), as well as those who are employees of a large national firm (wirehouses). While most of the statistics we will use and much of my personal experience come from the independent side of the industry, there is certainly no reason why a wirehouse team cannot apply the same concepts and techniques in their practice with some minor modifications to account for the factors they can manage as opposed to those managed by the home office (centralized management) of the firm.

The future belongs to ensembles. Ensemble practices have a demonstrated better ability to service clients well, to grow faster, and to attract the best talent. Opportunity is a cycle—firms that have opportunities attract talented people and create wealth. Wealth and people then create more opportunity and the cycle goes on until a drastic change in the firm or the business environment interrupts it. The success of the advisory industry in the last 10 years has attracted a lot of good people and a lot of capital to our industry. The time to capture that momentum is now and the best way to capture it is with a team of like-minded people. Let's examine together how you can do that.

## Notes

1. James Trager, "The People's Chronology," 1994.
2. Ibid.
3. Kathleen McBride, "The History of Financial Planning," AdvisorOne, December 1, 2005.
4. "2001 Financial Planning Association Survey of Financial Performance," published by Moss Adams LLP and sponsored by SEI Investments.
5. "The Say on Pay: Registered Reps 2011 Compensation Survey," *Registered Rep Magazine*, December 2011.
6. ibid.

7. James Green, "What's Your Practice Worth? FP Transitions' Latest Findings," AdvisorOne, October 2011.
8. "Real Deals 2010: Definitive Information on Mergers and Acquisitions for Advisors," published by Pershing Advisor Solutions and produced by FA Insight.
9. I should note that some acquirers see an opportunity in the conversion from a duplex to a single-family house, in other words, in helping the firm integrate.
10. "2011 Top Wealth Managers: Staffing and Survey Conclusions," AdvisorOne, August 2011.
11. Lorna Bourke, "Investment clients prefer one adviser backed by small team of experts: Survey, *New Model Adviser*, November 2007.
12. There are very large businesses like The Ritz Hotels and The Wynn Hotels that excel at that sense of "everyone is responsible" on a very large scale.
13. I will be assuming throughout the book that most readers are advisors interested in delivering a wealth management—oriented service to clients rather than only financial planning or just investment management.

# CHAPTER 2

# The Ensemble Structure

We defined ensemble firms as any team of professionals that service clients together and combine their skills, time, and expertise. The benefits of the team approach start with even the simplest of teams with just two professionals, and the positive effects amplify as the size of the team increases to bring even more capacity, expertise, and ideas. Indeed, ensemble firms exist of every possible kind—from a small advisory firm that just hired their first service advisor to the super-ensembles like Aspiriant with over 30 owner "operators."[1]

The different sizes create different organizational models and different levels of complexity that firms follow almost in an evolutionary pattern. Most ensemble firms start as either a vertical ensemble where one advisor is the lead and the other is the junior or associate or as a small partnership between two advisors. Over time, firms grow to expand the number of lead advisors, expand the ownership of the firm, and ultimately enter into a large and complex structure typically involving multiple teams of service professionals and a department-based structure as shown in Figure 2.1.

Each step of this growth has its own dominant theme that defines the firm at that stage of evolution. The first step is one of establishing reputation through accumulating a critical mass of clients to sustain the practice and enough presence so that referral sources are comfortable with the expertise of the firm. In other words, the first task is to establish the firm as no longer being a startup or "young." Before such reputation is established, it is practically impossible for the firm to progress into building a larger team and a more complex structure, unless it has a large reserve of capital and is able to "acquire reputation" by hiring experienced and well-regarded professionals.

Once the reputation has been established, firms usually embark on a process of defining their services and how those will be delivered in the

**FIGURE 2.1** Management Priorities and Phases of Growth

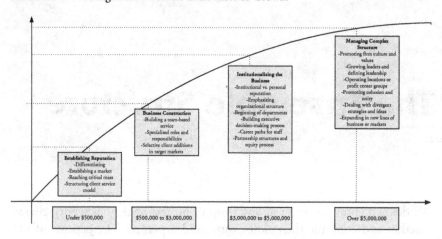

future. This service definition becomes the "molecule" of the new business and will persist for the next decade of the firm's development. The definition involves what the firm does and does not do, what people are involved in the servicing of a client, and how and what processes and systems are used. Later, the services may expand and the systems may be replaced, but the framework laid at this stage of business construction tends to persist and define the "DNA" of the firm for a long time. For example, if the firm establishes that each relationship will be serviced by a lead advisor, an associate, and a dedicated client services administrator, chances are that this structure will persist despite growth and other changes. Similarly, firms that at this stage choose to get involved with internal asset management tend to follow that service model for a long time.

Once the service model is established and the firm has accumulated a number of professionals who act as lead advisors, the focus shifts to institutionalizing the reputation of the firm so it is no longer Bob's firm or John's firm but rather relies on a real reputation that will drive the business development in the future. This process is slow, difficult, and requires tremendous patience and effort by the owners. Without it, though, the firm can never outgrow Bob and John, and often such firms struggle or disappear once the owners are gone or slow down.

There are relatively few super-ensembles—large firms with a large number of owner and nonowner advisors—but as independent firms are growing, we are likely to see more and more firms enter into this stage of complexity in their business. Complexity is indeed the key word in the management of super-ensembles as they examine which markets to enter into, how to segment their clients, how to manage the expectations of such a large group of professionals and partners, and how to continue to grow. Combining the emerging bureaucracy that the firm needs with the entrepreneurial spirit it is in danger of losing is a tricky task. Managing the culture of the firm in the absence of strong personal relationships (at this point some employees may not even know each other) is also one of the difficult tasks keeping the managing partners awake.

Let us examine each of the most typical ensemble structures with an eye toward the critical decisions the owners need to make, starting with the addition of a service advisor to a solo practice.

## The Service Advisor Model—Leverage

The most basic ensemble structure is one lead advisor supported by an associate who acts as a service advisor. Such a model is extremely common throughout all service industries—partner attorneys and associate attorneys, partner-level Certified Public Accountants (CPAs) and "manager" accountants, doctors and physician assistants, and so on The service advisor model offers the immediate advantage of leverage—that is, the ability to delegate work from a senior professional to one or more associate professionals who are qualified to complete the assignment and who receive lower levels of compensation. The result is not only increased capacity for the senior professional but also great economics.

For example, let's assume that an advisor needs approximately 20 hours to service the typical client relationship (this is close to the average shown by surveys[2]). Let's further assume that the advisor has about 1,600 hours available for working with clients (again close to what surveys show[3]). This means that the advisor has the theoretical capacity of approximately 80 clients to work with (80 × 20 = 1,600). Considering that the typical advisor in the industry is paid approximately $250,000 per year,[4] this means that each hour of the advisor's time is worth $156.25 ($250,000 in compensation divided by 1,600 hours). Now imagine the advisor could delegate 10 of the hours needed to a service advisor. This by itself will double the capacity of the team, since now the advisor can service 160 clients and the associate will absorb the additional 1,600 hours needed.

The increase in capacity comes also with great profitability. Let's assume each client pays the advisor exactly $5,000 in fees. An advisor who works alone will generate $5,000 × 80 = $400,000 in revenue. His or her compensation of $250,000 per year will consume 62.5 percent of the revenue—a high price ($250,000/$400,000). However, if the advisor was to hire an associate at a total compensation cost of $80,000 (close to the average shown in surveys[5]), he or she will double the revenue: 160 clients times $5,000 = $800,000, but the compensation cost will not increase proportionately—$250,000 (lead advisor) + $80,000 (service advisor) = $330,000 in total cost or 41.25 percent of the revenue. The practice doubled in size and went from 37.5 percent profit (100 percent less cost of 62.5 percent) to 58.75 percent profit (100 percent less 41.25 percent). This economic effect is called "leverage" for its ability to amplify the income-generating capacity of a senior advisor. In some extreme cases, I have worked with advisors who use three or even four associates for every senior professional achieving tremendous leverage, although those cases are very rare.

It is much more typical to see a structure such as the one in Figure 2.2 where one lead advisor works with one service professional and a couple of operations/admin employees. Such a structure creates leverage while maintaining consistency of service and involvement from the senior professional. It delivers the desired economic effect without sacrificing much of the personal relationship between the senior advisor and the client that is so important for client retention.

This structure of one lead advisor with one service advisor is not only an evolutionary step in the growth of an ensemble firm but it is also a critical building block for all the large firms in the industry. Even in the largest ensemble firms, the client service is still organized around this same delivery team. It not only contains the right mix of capacity and economics, but it also creates a mentoring relationship that allows for the growth of the service professionals into lead advisors.

**FIGURE 2.2**  Typical Vertical Ensemble Structure

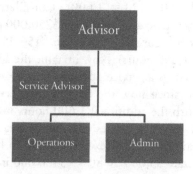

Many ensembles use this structure as a step on their growth path. Usually, firms that have revenue between $500,000 and $1,000,000 start to consider the addition of a service advisor, and this is very often the first service professional that joins the solo owner of the firm and turns it into an ensemble practice. We will discuss this growth path in more detail in the next chapter.

The lead advisor and service advisor structure is also an excellent potential succession vehicle. As service advisors progress in their career and professional development they often become lead advisors themselves and are capable of fully absorbing the responsibility for the clients. Thus, if someday the lead advisor has the desire to fully or partially retire, he or she can rely on another professional who is familiar with the clients to take over. No one is in a better position to take over the practice than an advisor who has been working with the same clients for years. Naturally, the assumption is that the service advisor will be younger in years than the lead advisor, and therefore they will retire at different times.

The critical decisions facing an advisor who is interested in creating an ensemble through this leverage (vertical) structure are:

- **Can you define specific roles and responsibilities for a service professional in your firm?** There is no benefit to hiring someone to "watch" you work without a significant and consistent workload. Such an addition will burden the expenses of the practice and will also leave you with an individual that is wondering what he or she is actually doing to contribute (or getting used to doing nothing).
- **Do you have a well-defined service process that another person can follow?** Practices that rely on the advisor to apply "virtuoso" improvisation skills have a very difficult time adding another professional to the client relationship. Whenever I hear an advisor say, "I listen to the client and then act according to their needs," I am always asking myself if that means "I go to the meeting and play it by ear." Nothing wrong with playing it by ear, but most inexperienced people need the sheet music in order to follow.
- **Can you provide a career path and are you comfortable with letting "another cook in your kitchen"?** While some individuals are comfortable being in a support role for their entire career, most professionals dream of being an advisor. "There is a general's baton in every soldier's backpack," says Napoleon. When that general emerges, you, as the lead advisor, will have to be comfortable giving them the chance to practice with their own clients and letting them define their own service.

Otherwise you are likely either to work only with underperforming individuals or to face a revolving door of frustrated service advisors.

- **Can you hold yourself accountable?** Needless to say, when you have another person involved in your client service process, you need to be more accountable to the process itself as well as to the person working at your side.
- **Can you afford it?** The reason why this ensemble structure is typical for larger firms is the affordability factor. To add another sizeable salary and the accompanying benefits and taxes, you will need to create the necessary workload and financial capacity.

## The Emerging Partnerships—Sharing

If the key word for vertical ensembles is "leverage" (as in leveraging the time of the senior advisor), the key word for small partnerships is "sharing" (as in sharing everything). There is no size limit for creating a partnership and there is no service process or organizational engineering necessary—the magic is simply "Share!" If two or three advisors can agree to share office space, office equipment, technology systems, office expenses, branding, staff, revenues, client relationships, and potentially profits (in order of importance and difficulty) they can create a powerful ensemble structure that can enhance both practices. In fact, some of the top firms in the industry started as partnerships between two advisors with a lot of ambition and very little revenue.

We will differentiate the small partnerships discussed in this section and shown in Figure 2.3 from their larger brethren—the "true" ensembles

**FIGURE 2.3** Typical Ensemble Partnership Structure

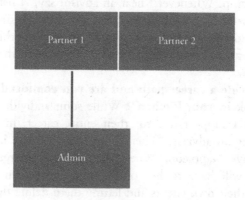

and the "super" ensembles—simply so we can focus on the critical decisions facing the emerging stage of a partnership practice. Once the partners also leverage themselves and add service advisors to the mix, we will call that a "true" ensemble (true because it combines the sharing and the leverage) and will discuss it in the next section.

There is a reason why most emerging partnerships are formed between advisors who are just starting in the business—when you have nothing, you have less to argue over! In the beginning of a practice, creating relationships with clients and referral sources is the paramount goal, and advisors are willing to subjugate their ego and their preferences to that goal. Enthusiasm is also high and inertia is nonexistent. No one is "set in their ways" and thus there are no conflicts of the ways between the two new partners. Finally, both are equally starved for income, and there is a certain camaraderie in poverty that makes sharing easier.

The sharing of resources between the partners takes on different forms and therefore creates a variety of arrangements, but the sharing process starts with office space and then expands to more involved areas of the practice.

## Sharing Office Space

Sharing office space is very common in the industry and allows advisors to share the liability of the lease, access better space, as well as share the features of the space that will be otherwise difficult to obtain for a small firm—for example, conference rooms, reception desk, and so on. This kind of arrangement is very far from the ensemble concept we are discussing, but it can be the starting point of a deeper relationship. As my friend and partner Stuart Silverman likes to say, "Before you share a house and kids with a girl you want to try sharing the french fries on a date."

Such sharing arrangements appear to be very easy to negotiate and structure, but there are a surprising number of issues that pop up. When entering into such sharing arrangements it is always a good idea to (1) prepare a letter or even a contract that details your arrangement and have both sides accept it in writing; (2) be specific in your arrangement about the details—decide what resources you can use, what portion of the assistants' time you can rely on, and so on; (3) specify who has the lease liability, whether you can split that liability, and what happens if one of you leaves; (4) state how you will make decisions about investing in the space, for example, buying a new copy machine; and (5) decide who is the employer and manager of shared employees and how you will manage them together.

I often hear advisors discuss economies of scale as one of the positive effects of partnering with another advisor. "Economies of scale" refers to the ability to leverage a fixed expense (e.g., a copy machine) over more revenue or more use—for example, sharing the copy machine between two practices rather than each advisor buying his or her own. While economies of scale certainly seem like a logical result of the sharing arrangement, we should be realistic about the extent of such cost advantage. Unfortunately, the scale is not very significant and does not extend much further beyond some simple office equipment and perhaps splitting one assistant. In other words, the advisor contemplating a partnership should not expect more than $5,000 to $10,000 in economic benefit compared to doing this on his or her own. Realistically, the "hassle" factor, that is, the cost of accommodating each other, is probably higher than the cost savings.

Where true benefits lie is not so much in the scale but the scope—that ability to access better resources together than you can on your own. For example, you may be able to rent better space if you partner up (offices under 1,000 square feet are not as abundant and many are subleases). You may be able to purchase a better Client Relationship Management system (CRM) system if you buy more "seats," and most of all, you may be able to attract a better quality of talent in a larger office.

## Sharing a Brand Name

The long sequence of names on the door has always been the stereotype for a law firm,[6] but advisors are learning fast, and I have seen a few doors that are covered by a small-font sign of a long name. Advisors are surprisingly easy-going when it comes to changing their brand and combining names. Next to sharing space, I actually see this partnership arrangement most often. It is very common to see two advisors, say, Joe Stock and Peter Bond, combine their branding under "Stock & Bond Advisors" but essentially have nothing else in common. Usually Joe will have his own clients and staff and Peter will have his own, and the two gentlemen often do not even share space.

Creating the impression of a large practice through this "name change" process is a viable option, but it is a little bit like getting married for the green card—it is easy to do, but then you have to live with it for quite a while. That said, the effects on clients and prospects is usually positive. I have worked with many practices who report that clients welcome the new "partnership." You have to remember, though, that clients are really attracted to the fact that you have a partner and therefore more depth and a broader pool of knowledge. Sooner or later they will realize that

"Advisory Associates" is nothing but a name. A client a long time ago whose firm's name was Durst and Associates told me how clients will ask him, "Doug, we see you, but where are the associates?" He had none at the time, but Doug later built a fantastic large practice. That's the point—behaving like a large firm in the early stages of your history, including having a large firm name, can be very helpful, but sooner or later reality has to catch up with the story.

## Sharing Staff

Sharing staff is perhaps the border between a silo arrangement and a true partnership. I guess if you have kids together, you are a couple! Not to compare employees to kids, but if a relationship has evolved to the point where the partners are jointly responsible for the performance, compensation, and careers of several people, they can share and work together on all aspects of the business.

Sharing staff proves very difficult since the two practices coming together have not only very different needs and processes but likely different cultures and personality styles. The employees thus have to learn to work with two very different types of communications style and often different set of expectations. In a solo practice, performance is often measured as "what Bob likes!" In a partnership, you have to define the expectations and have a more objective set of expectations. The responsibility of providing compensation (financial) and a career (ethical) to a set of people also tends to almost force the partners to work together and often becomes the catalyst for the ensemble formation.

## Sharing Clients and Profits

Sharing clients and sharing profits are practically synonymous—I have never seen a partnership in which advisors share responsibility for the clients but do not share profits. The reason is straightforward: The clients are the source of all revenues and therefore profits—I guess if you share the cows you share the milk! I did not want to compare clients to milking cows; these parallels sometimes just run away from me. We will discuss the process of sharing clients and profits in detail in Chapter 5.

Finally, if it is not clear to this point, I don't believe that long-term silo arrangements work. They tend to create friction and conflict, they are short lived, they are usually less efficient than each practice operating on its own, and they tend to set the wrong tone with the staff. Finally, they tend to affect your thinking about partnerships in general—many advisors are scarred by bad partnerships where they suffered aggravation and/or losses in the hands of a partner. Usually that was not a real partner but rather a silo arrangement that fell apart.

We will discuss the process of merging practices together in great detail in Chapter 4, but in summary, the critical decisions facing an advisor who is interested in creating an ensemble through such emerging partnership are the following:

- Why are you partnering? What can you do together that you can't do on your own?
- Do you practice in a compatible way and with compatible clients?
- Do you share similar ambitions and a similar vision for the future?
- Do you trust and respect the other professional?
- Are you open to modifying your practice to create room for another professional?
- Are you open to being vulnerable to the actions of a partner in exchange for benefiting from the actions of a partner?
- What is your history with partnerships, and is that history influencing your view? How likely is that history to repeat in this case?

## The "True" Ensembles—Leverage and Sharing Combined

When the power of leverage and sharing combine, ensemble practices demonstrate their strength and reach their peak growth and profitability. Practices arrive at this destination on different paths—some start as a small partnership that grows to the point where the two partners hire a service advisor. Others start as one lead advisor and one service advisor who over time becomes a lead advisor himself or herself. The history often determines the skill set—practices that started as partnerships tend to be good at sharing and making decisions together, practices that evolved through leverage tend to be good at growing people. To succeed as a true ensemble, though, all practices will have to become good at both.

Most firms reach this stage at around $1 million in revenue. There is no magic to this number, but it tends to generate enough income to the partners while allowing a budget for the hiring of at least one service professional. The distribution of ownership can also vary significantly—many practices are equal partnerships between the two or three founders while just as many have one founding majority partner and multiple minority partners. In all

**FIGURE 2.4**   Typical Large Ensemble Partnership Structure

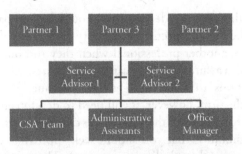

forms of ownership, however, there is a distinct shift from working with specific people (Bob, John, Scott) to working with a position (lead advisor, service advisor, etc.). The specific person gives way to the more abstract notion of a position, and the advisor positions take center stage in that process.

## Managing Advisors

My former partner Cathy Gibson used to describe managing professionals as "herding cats." As difficult as that process may be, though, it is essential for the success of an ensemble firm. As you can see in Figure 2.4, three or more partners will have to come together to manage a firm, its employees, and its client relationships. There are several components to that process:

- Creating and managing job descriptions.
- Developing a system of accountability for the service and financial results.
- Establishing a training and mentoring process for the more junior professionals.
- Synchronizing the service process between the partners to allow for sharing of services and advisors and other resources.
- Formalizing investment decision making.
- Developing a clear professional career path and defining the compensation associated with each step of the process.

We will discuss each of these factors in detail in the next chapter, but we still want to highlight the cultural transition, though in the early stages of a business, the business accommodates the people. In a mature business, the people accommodate the business. This is the stage of growth where you as an advisor will have to start accommodating your firm.

## How Many Service Advisors to Hire?

The staffing of the advisory department should be approached from two potentially conflicting perspectives—capacity and talent development. In general, firms hire another professional when they run out of capacity and need help. This also assures that they can afford the new salary—especially in the service positions that do not generate revenue. For the long-term development of the firm, however, it will need to develop and add a cadre of professionals perhaps beyond the immediate capacity need.

My rule of thumb is that you should seek approximately $500,000 in revenue per professional (including the owners). Thus you can hire another advisor when you exceed a million in revenue and you have two advisors (say, you and your partner). This will cause your ratio to drop below $500,000 temporarily, but hopefully balance will be quickly restored. On the other hand, if you wait till your firm reaches $1,500,000 in revenue to hire a third person, you will spend a lot of time being stretched beyond your capacity. Such rules of thumb can be dangerous, though—there are many good reasons to deviate significantly from these ratios—for example, the size of the typical client relationships, the strategy of the firm, the services it offers, the presence of internal investment management capabilities, and so on.

The reason to "overstaff" with advisors is that it takes a significant amount of time to train and coach service advisors on the specific process used by the firm. It may take as much as a year until a service advisor is fully productive. Thus if you hire staff when you are overwhelmed, you will need to wait another year until you get help.

The other issue is the risk of losing talent. Even in the best managed firms, there is always the danger of losing employees to life events—people marry, move to other cities, change their minds, pursue new careers, have kids, get sick, and so forth. There is no way to isolate the firm against such events, and if you are only relying on one service professional for the future of the firm, you may be exposed to a significant risk. Having depth at the position isolates you against such losses.

Finally, people tend to learn better in groups. Hiring and training a class of advisors together leverages the training effort but also creates a learning environment and camaraderie. Advisors from the same class tend to help one another, learn from one another, and provide one another with emotional support—a very important factor for success. Large accounting firms understand this process and implement it exceptionally well. The early career relationships often last for the rest of the career of the professionals that grew together. A younger advisor who is the only one at this level of experience can often feel isolated and discouraged and will have a difficult time relating his or her concerns to the more senior people. Some of those concerns may simply not be for the ears of a supervisor.

In other words, there is a significant benefit to hiring aggressively in the development positions. This creates depth of talent immediately available for growth and also provides for a better training environment. Sometimes, the service advisors can also help train less experienced colleagues.

## Is There a Place for a Third Level of Advisor?

So far we have been discussing a structure with a lead advisor and a service advisor—the lead is the relationship manager and business developer, and the service advisor does all the portfolio and planning work and also works with the client on the more routine implementation. Many firms, however, use a third level of professional—an entry-level position often referred to as "paraplanner," "associate advisor," or "junior advisor." This is usually a position that is on a clear path to being an advisor but lacks the experience to service clients independently. Often the responsibilities are overlapping with a client service administrator but with clear focus on the professional work.

Frequently, associate advisors have less than three years of experience, and very often their work focuses on plan drafts and portfolio analysis since those tasks require less client interaction but more technical knowledge than administrative staff have.

The use of a three-level process (lead, service, associate) is largely dependent on the size of the typical client relationship—if a firm works with large client relationships, on average there is usually enough meaningful work and enough financial resources to leverage to this point. On smaller client relationships, though, the amount of time spent delegating may potentially outweigh the benefits of the leverage.

If you could only hire one professional and you had to choose between a service advisor position (can service existing clients independently) and an associate position (can only perform professional tasks but not work with a client independently), I would almost always chose a service advisor. The leverage effect created significantly outweighs the difference in compensation. However, if you have the economics and service model to afford both levels, the combined leverage and the training process created will benefit your firm a lot. Service advisors are also less available and more difficult to

**FIGURE 2.5**  Typical Large Ensemble Department Structure

recruit, as many firms recognize how productive they can be. Finally, the real world is never as clear as the world of organizational charts—many job candidates have a mix of experience that puts them somewhere in the middle—for example, very strong technical skills but underdeveloped relationship skills. This is perhaps the biggest advantage of large firms—their ability to recruit and provide careers to talented people of various experience and skills.

## Departments

In the larger ensemble structure, there will be groups of job descriptions who perform together with a distinctly separate decision-making and management process. In other words, large ensembles (over $1 billion in client assets) should start thinking about departments. A department structure allows more focused and responsive decision making and specialization in the management function. Figure 2.5 shows a simplistic schematic of the typical departments that emerge.

At some point it is simply not practical to have all partners making all decisions It is much more efficient to specialize in expertise—chances are that not all partners are knowledgeable on all the issues that require a decision. Resources can also be allocated with more clear accountability with a department structure—you can measure performance and accountability easier within a department. Last but not least, the departments allow a firm to assign leaders to each function—the people who will make the critical decisions and provide the staff in that department with the necessary career and job guidance.

Typically the departments that appear first are the following:

- **Operations Department**—This department incorporates the client service administration functions—performance reporting, trading, client data and account management, custodian and broker-dealer interface, record management, and so on, and internal administration—accounting, administrative assistance, human resources (HR), internal information technology (IT), and so forth. The department is sometimes led by one of the partners who has an interest in operations but more often by an office manager whose job has grown with the firm.

- **Investment Department**—Even firms that do not manage assets internally tend to develop investment departments that include the positions focused on research, portfolio construction, portfolio management, and investment decisions. The department often starts with a single individual, but depending on the strategy of the firm, it can grow quickly. The presence of such a department is usually a strong statement that the strategy of the firm will emphasize investment sophistication and potentially investment returns.
- **Planning Department**—There are two types of firms that develop planning departments—firms that do a lot of planning and firms that do very little planning. Firms that construct sophisticated comprehensive plans usually find it more efficient to dedicate a specialist to that task. As the firm grows the single professional may be joined by others forming a department. On the opposite side of the spectrum, firms that do little planning may isolate the function with a single specialist. In that case the department rarely grows past a single individual.
- **Tax Department**—The presence of a tax department is usually a staple of a firm with a CPA background (there are many firms in the industry that spun away from CPA firms) or a family office.
- **Insurance Department**—There are many wealth management firms in the industry who started with strong roots in insurance and who have as a result significant insurance revenues, and therefore they staff a full-fledged department focused on this service.

The development of departments is a necessary and constructive organizational step. To avoid turning it into a cumbersome and detracting feature, though, advisors need to make sure that departments don't become "firms within the firm" and that each department receives the attention of the leaders of the firm. This is particularly true for operations where there is a real danger of splitting between a front office and a back office. Operations is also an area that advisors often prefer not to focus on, and so the operations department often becomes the "stepchild."

As the ensemble firm grows and reaches new highs in revenues and staff, the complexity of the structure increases until we reach the next stage of development, which we will call "super-ensemble."

## The Super-Ensemble Firms

Once a firm grows past $1 billion in assets under management and/or has over 30 employees, it enters into a different level of organizational complexity and management practices. If the first three stages of organizational growth were defined by the interpersonal relationships between advisors—sharing, delegating, managing, and so on—the super-ensemble firms take on a more abstract organizational form that is more in line with traditional corporate organization. Departments are fully developed and have well-defined decision-making and operating procedures. There are multiple levels of management and much time and attention is devoted to the way the organization administers itself.

The management of such large organizational form is not the focus of this book and deserves its own specialized text with many complex topics to be discussed. That said, since some of the management issues facing super-ensembles also affect smaller ensembles, I would like to go through several topics that tend to present super-ensemble owners with critical decisions, namely, having multiple lines of business, the ability to establish multiple locations, and finally using the operational capabilities of the firm as a platform for recruiting other professionals.

### Multiple Lines of Business

Super-ensemble firms often embark on separate lines of business such as (in order of frequency) investment management for clients of other advisors, investment consulting for institutional clients, retirement planning and retirement benefits, insurance services, tax services, and the like. The premise behind such an expansion is one of the following:

- Distribution strategy—Existing clients demand and benefit from additional services—for example, tax planning or insurance—and the client relationship gives the firm a competitive advantage. Of course, many firms started first with the second service and then expanded into wealth management (CPA firms buying wealth managers, benefits firms adding an RIA, etc.).
- Leveraging a resource—This primarily applies to the investment department. The high-cost investment department is theoretically easily leveraged by offering the same strategies to third-party clients. "Theoretically" because in reality this strategy is very difficult to execute.

To succeed with multiple lines of business a firm will have to have critical mass to compete in each business, leadership in each business, and a clear synergy between the businesses that is enforced by the firm culture and espoused by all partners. Unfortunately, most of the time one or more of these factors is not present, and one of the businesses is underperforming and creating a distraction for everyone in the firm. There is no shortage of synergistic opportunities in the market, but the critical mass component is often underestimated, especially in the case of investment management offered as a separate business. Firms underestimate the amount of resources and staff necessary to *distribute* an investment product as opposed to *creating* one. Every grandma can cook a spaghetti sauce in her own kitchen, but selling spaghetti sauce in a jar at the supermarket is a different game altogether.

There is also often lack of agreement between the partners on a multiproduct strategy, but one partner is passionate about it, so the others indulge him—long term that is rarely a recipe for success. The partner who is driving the strategy by himself or herself usually feels isolated and lacks resources.

In other words, while there are many opportunities to develop additional services, such opportunities should be viewed with constructive skepticism. The questions should be—does it support our strategy, do we have the resources, do we have a leader, can we focus on this? For most ensemble firms and most of the time the answer will be "No!" but still superensembles have an advantage in pursuing such opportunities.

## Multiple Locations

Establishing multiple physical locations without losing your identity as a firm and maintaining the same culture and strategy has always been the Achilles heel of service firms. The physical separation creates a completely different flow of information and decision making, which usually results in each location becoming a "tribe" within the larger nation. This is not necessarily a problem in itself, but unfortunately the tribal differences usually turn into differences in (1) compensation, (2) service delivery, (3) operations, and (4) profitability, and pretty soon each tribe prefers to retain its own ways and its own resources. When this process continues unchecked, the meaning of being part of the same firm often disappears.

To make matters worse, remote offices that don't have strong leadership tend to falter and crumble by turning people over and losing clients. On the other hand, offices with strong leadership tend to splinter and tribalize. In other words, the rock and the hard place are waiting. The solution may lie in creating strong leaders in the hub and sending them out to disperse the culture and the ways of the mother ship. In some ways, that is what large empires like those of ancient Rome and China used to do— groom and educate the future provincial leaders in the capital and indoctrinate them close to the capital so that they could become the link to the central culture rather than remain barbarian chieftains. In the context of an advisory firm, that means establishing a very strong central office with tremendous depth of talent and becoming adept at relocating that talent to the satellite offices.

## The Firm as a Platform or a Franchise

At a certain size and geographic dispersion the firm may start acting more as an operations platform than as an actual cohesive unit of activity and strategy. There are firms in the industry that while they are owned and operated as ensemble partnerships have such size and physical distance between the practice offices that they start resembling independent broker-dealers, like Raymond James and Commonwealth, or technology platforms like Fortigent. Combined with firm-wide branding efforts, the result may resemble a franchise in the sense that each office behaves independently and retains the majority of its economics, but there is some adherence to the brand that keeps the firms together.

Advisors who are looking to join such a firm should understand that there is a tremendous difference between the world of partnerships we have discussed to this point and the culture and operations of a firm of this type. Without implying any criticism in this statement I believe that "platform" firms tend to resemble wirehouse firms like Merrill Lynch and UBS. Ultimately, advisors receive an outstanding quality of support and operations but find that they need to operate in the confines of the operating and financial space provided by the firm. Similarly, the human resource support is outstanding and recruiting people to your team is easier, but at the same time the ability to create your own culture and control your own environment is severely diminished. Unfortunately, this type of firm usually comes with complex internal politics and is always under the threat of change of ownership. That said, if you want to be an owner in an advisory firm but you do not want to participate in the process of managing the firm and you want to focus on your clients, this may be a great solution for you.

## When Large Becomes Too Large

Very few advisory firms are at a stage where they have to worry about becoming too large and bureaucratic, but for some reason many business owners are worried about this issue. I guess this is a manifestation of the intensely independent nature of the advisors—to them one of the worst things that can happen to their business is to turn it into a bank-like corporation. The answer really depends on the ambition and personality of the people involved—some advisors want to build empires that are as large as the market will allow, and others want to preserve the spirit of entrepreneurship and the ability to control the firm and their own balance of life.

Still, for those that want to know where they are in the growth spectrum, I will offer the following simple test:

- The day when the firm has a client you have never met before is the day when you have a true ensemble practice.
- The day when you have an employee you have never met before is the day when you have a super-ensemble—a very large firm.
- The day when you have a partner you have never met before is perhaps the day when your firm has become too large.

With that said, let's take a look at how you can get to the stage where you have a client you have never met!

## Notes

1. A term used by the firm itself.
2. "Practice Update 2007: Time Management and Personal Productivity," AdvisorImpact.
3. Ibid.
4. "2011 Moss Adams/Investment News Adviser Compensation and Staffing Study," Moss Adams, reports median pretax income per advisor of $262,781.
5. "2011 Moss Adams/Investment News Adviser Compensation and Staffing Study," Moss Adams, reports median total cash compensation of $81,686.
6. According to a *Wall Street Journal* blogger, the longest law firm name is Ziffren, Brittenham, Branca, Fischer, Gilbert-Lurie, Stiffelman, Cook, Johnson, Lande & Wolf. You have to feel for Wolf—he or she is last in line.

# CHAPTER 3

# Growing into an Ensemble

When you arrive at the conclusion that you want to build an ensemble practice, you will find that hiring professionals with less experience and helping them grow into lead advisors is perhaps the most reliable and most available path to building an institutionalized, valuable, large firm. Partnering, merging, and acquiring a practice each have their merits, but they require finding a potential merger or acquisition partner (scarce) and working through a complex set of compromises and accommodations of the other party. In contrast, hiring and grooming professionals allows you to control the process, work with a large available pool of candidates, and ultimately fashion the culture of the firm over your own values and practice model. However, it requires patience, dedication to coaching other professionals, and willingness to work through the inevitable disappointments. For the success of this strategy, you need to identify the right time to hire, the right person to hire, and the right set of responsibilities for the new professional or professionals. Let's discuss each of those factors.

## The Right Time to Hire

The right time to add a professional to your firm has to do with three criteria—(1) being able to afford the compensation cost, (2) having structured your client work to the point where you can delegate some of it, and

(3) being emotionally ready to add another "cook in the kitchen." Let's discuss each of these factors in turn:

- **When you can afford the compensation cost**. From an affordability standpoint the practice should be ready for a service professional once you reach $500,000 in revenue. It's not that hiring a service advisor is unadvisable under that level of revenue, but it will likely significantly reduce the income to the owner—perhaps below what is needed for his or her personal life. This is an important concept we will elaborate on in Chapter 11—how much income do you need to support your personal life? Knowing that income number will allow you to "invest" the surplus income in the practice.

    Typically, a practice with $500,000 in revenue will have overhead of $120,000 to $150,000—most of it will consist of the salary of one administrative assistant and the rent for the office. This leaves the owners with $380,000 to $350,000 in pretax income. Needless to say, income and other taxes will likely consume a third of that income, leaving the owner with after-tax income of around $240,000 (rounding and approximating). This is where the personal income needs come into play. If the owner needs $180,000 in personal after-tax income, then he or she has about $60,000 ($240,000 available less $180,000 needed) to invest in the compensation of a service advisor. You may note that the compensation of the employee will be a before-tax expense and therefore your budget will be "magnified" by the 33 percent we initially set aside for taxes. However, you also have to account for payroll taxes and potentially benefits. A new employee will also add to your overhead (computer, consumables, etc.) and potentially require you to increase your rented space.

    Investing beyond the level of income you need to pay personal expenses will put too much pressure on you as a business owner. You will need to grow the practice rapidly and the pressure may make you very vulnerable to a decline in the market.

    Being able to afford another employee is not the same as achieving optimal economics though—that will happen later when your firm grows. Ideally, the combination of your compensation as an owner (give yourself a salary of $150,000 + $50,000 in other compensation = $200,000 if unsure what compensation you should have) and the salary of the service advisor should ideally equal 40 percent of the revenue of the practice (or less). This means that you will need $200,000 for your salary + $80,000 salary and other costs for the new employee advisor = $280,000/40 percent of revenue = $700,000 in revenue. Or in other words, when you reach

$700,000 in revenue, the professional compensation will be at the optimal 40 percent level.

- **When you have structured your client service.** Chefs in most restaurants have prep-cooks or sous chefs—the exact same concept of leverage we have been discussing. In order to hire another chef in the kitchen, though, you have to write out your recipes. No chefs can help you cook if they don't know how you prepare a beef bourguignon. They may have studied this classical dish in cooking school, but they will have no idea of your individual additions to the recipe. In other words, before you get help you need to get organized.

  At minimum you will need to identify the major activities in the firm (Table 3.1 will help you do that) and describe in a bullet point list the steps for accomplishing the task. You will likely have to then articulate what part of the process will be run by the service professional and what part will be done by you or the operations staff. It is always a great idea to involve your operations staff in this process too—this will help them in their work with the service advisor.

- **When you have prepared emotionally.** It is not easy letting another cook in your kitchen, even if they just chop vegetables. My wife and I drive each other crazy when we try to cook together—turns out it is easier to share your entire life with someone than to cook a pork-shoulder. Perhaps this highlights the difference between thinking of your practice as a family kitchen and treating it as a restaurant.

  We have all become so accustomed to the saying that there are "too many cooks in the kitchen" that we assume that there can be only one chef in the kitchen. This is where we are getting confused—we are thinking of grandma's kitchen and not a large restaurant. A restaurant always has multiple chefs in the kitchen, and it is time to start thinking like a restaurant. This is a key decision—are you ready to become a restaurant or do you prefer to just "cook" home-style?

## Whom Can You Hire?

There are over 300,000 individuals in the United States who practice as financial advisory professionals,[1] and there is certainly no shortage of new professionals coming into the industry. The success of the industry has turned it from a well-kept secret to a magnet for recent college graduates and many career changers. This means that as the owner of a practice looking to hire a professional, you will have a choice from a very deep pool of candidates.

There are three characteristics of the candidates that you will have to choose from, each characteristic presenting you with a continuum of experience and expertise:

1. **Technical skills and theoretical knowledge**—this describes their knowledge of financial planning theory, modern portfolio theory and other investment theory, their knowledge of products, analytical skills, and experience, and their knowledge of the software and other tools used in the industry.
2. **Client relationship skill**—the ability to relate to clients, establish and maintain a relationship, gauge client satisfaction, understand how to explore and uncover needs, and the ability to tackle difficult questions and situations, including reacting to criticism and fixing mistakes.
3. **Business development skills**—the ability to market on behalf of the firm, generate leads independently, work with qualified leads to propose services, and ultimately convert prospects to clients.

The tendency for most business owners is to look for someone who can "bring some business," but we have to go back to the nature of your first advisor hire—you are looking for someone to help you create leverage and service existing clients, not necessarily another salesperson. What is more, professionals who can develop business are rarely available as employees— they tend to seek ownership and fall more in the category of mergers discussed in the next chapter. Given the different combinations of the three skills described above, there are generally several categories of professionals available:

- Entry-level professional—According to the Financial Planning Association (FPA) over 5,100[2] new Certified Financial Planner applicants sat for the exam for the first time in 2011 alone. They are eager to get started and score highly on the theoretical knowledge scale. Unfortunately, many have no experience in working with clients and are at least 10 years away from any business development. Such hires are a great opportunity for the larger firms who have an established training process, have three layers of leverage (entry-level professionals have a hard time becoming service advisors immediately), and have the culture that can welcome young people and quickly indoctrinate them. With those factors present, the cost of such professionals allows for a great return on investment and within three to four years they can develop into very capable service advisors.

- Technicians—There is also a cadre of professionals who have been in a technical role in another firm for a period of time. This includes professionals who have been investment analysts, planners, and investment researchers in a firm and may have many years of experience in that role but wish to become advisors. Again, the technical skills may be very high but the client and business development skills very low. Unlike the entry-level employees, technicians may be very easy to find a role for in a firm of any size—they can absorb capably many functions while learning to become better relationship managers. Unfortunately their compensation expectations are often unreasonable for the training required—they have history of compensation significantly exceeding what firms pay service professionals. If the compensation, however, is agreeable, technicians are a terrific hire for any firm.
- Service professional—There are certainly also professionals who are already in a service role with another firm and may be looking to change firms. This is certainly a dream hire with perfect experience and usually reasonable compensation expectations. Such opportunities are very rare, though—less than 5 percent of all service professionals look to change firms[3] as the best performers at the service advisor position are closely guarded employees who receive a lot of attention from their firm. Without being too cynical, when you encounter such prospective employees you should always ask yourself if they struggled with performance in their previous firm. Of course there are plenty of firms that are mismanaged and do not provide opportunity to their employees; they will therefore be great firms to recruit from.
- Disappointed broker—The large wirehouse firms and insurance organizations continue to hire and then let go thousands of entry-level professionals. During their tenure in the corporate organization they receive varying degrees of training and experience—some develop fantastic technical skills, work as service advisors, and complete their licensing and professional designations. Others simply try to survive and put together a practice and receive no training. What is worse, they also often develop bad habits—most of all a product-oriented mentality and difficulty sharing clients with another advisor. In other words, these are potentially good candidates but require careful evaluation and in-depth interviewing. They also come with the wrong frame of reference with respect to pay. Many candidates look for a stable income but also do not want to forgo the payout structure completely as they have seen how it can lead to high income. This is obviously not practical for an independent business, but

somehow quite a few owners have talked themselves into packages such as $50,000 salary + 30 percent payout—a clear mistake. We will repeat this several times in the compensation chapter, but you should never cater compensation to a specific candidate—it should rather cater to the position.

- Mid-level broker—Advisors who survive the wirehouse or insurance "house cleanings" but still fall very low on the production grids often apply for service positions. They usually have as much as $200,000 in revenue, making them an attractive hire from an affordability perspective since they have their own revenue base. However, this category also presents significant challenges. Advisors in this category have trouble seeing themselves as purely service professionals since they have already been a lead advisor on some relationships; on the other hand, they are not ready to be a full-time lead as they do not have enough revenue and lead-generation ability. As a result, you often get the complications and compensation expectations of a lead advisor with the skills of a service professional.
- Career changers—I have worked with many firms who have converted a client into an employee and done so successfully. There are many professionals who after a good career in the corporate world look to practice as an advisor, drawn by the interactivity of the profession and the flexibility of working in a small business. Career changers often have outstanding client skills and even lead-generation ability but relatively low technical skills. They are very intriguing prospects for service advisors but often bring a very incompatible set of expectations and compensation history. Many have had salaries well into the $200,000s and $300,000s and have trouble going back to the five-digit compensation packages that prevail for service advisors.
- Experienced broker—Finally, occasionally experienced brokers will show interest in service positions. In my mind such opportunities fall more in the merger category and should be discussed in that context. In other words—see Chapter 4.

So after we have extensively catalogued the potential candidates, who are the best candidates for a practice to hire? The answer will depend on your strategy and your needs. Every group of candidates has its own set of advantages and challenges and obviously every candidate will need to be evaluated on their own merit. Within every group, there are individuals of varying talent and motivation so careful interviewing is necessary part of the process.

## Structuring Client Service

There are two underlying assumptions behind our approach to using the service advisor position:

1. It is a position that should be productive and contribute to the success of the firm from day one. The service advisor is not an apprentice, whose development is subsidized by the owners of the firm. The position is part of the client service team with important contribution to the service process.
2. The ideal outcome for the service advisor position is to develop into a lead advisor. Therefore progress and training opportunities are very important. Not every service advisor will turn into a lead advisor and that's okay. However, if the firm is never able to help a service advisor progress to the lead position, it will eventually be very constraint in its growth.

Based on these two assumptions, the job description of a service advisor should be a carefully structured combination of contributing to client service and training opportunities. Every firm will have a different combination of responsibilities, but Table 3.1 presents my attempt at generalizing the activities that the service advisor can take over. Some activities may be handled by two levels—for example, both service advisors and operations staff will be involved in routine service requests such as wiring cash to the client. Others, though, will be the exclusive domain of the service advisor.

Most of all, I believe service advisors can focus on relationship management, the periodic reviews of established plans and portfolios, and the data analysis that goes into the planning decisions. They should also be present in all the meetings with clients and should be looking for opportunities to expand the relationship, including assets that are not managed by the firm or needs such as estate planning. Where service advisors can have less contribution but should eventually contribute to is the area of business development and marketing. Those areas should be part of their growth plan but will be difficult to develop from the start.

Finally, it is not always easy to distinguish between the responsibilities of a client service administrator and a service advisor—there is a lot of overlap and duplicate tasks. That should not be a problem and in fact it is good to have some redundancy in the client service process. Where the distinction between the positions lies, is that the service advisor is responsible for

**TABLE 3.1** Typical Division of Responsibilities in an Ensemble Firm

| | Lead Advisor | Service Advisors | Operations |
|---|---|---|---|
| Building Awareness and Reputations | X | | |
| Generating Leads | X | | |
| Proposal and Sales | X | | |
| New Sales to Existing Clients | X | X | |
| Initial Analysis, Recommendations, and Setup (portfolio and plan) | X | X | |
| Relationship Management | X | X | |
| Periodic Reviews | | X | |
| Strategic Changes in the Plan and Relationship | X | | |
| Maintaining Data and Accounts | | | X |
| Routine Services | | X | X |
| Answering Basic Questions and Requests | | X | X |
| Crisis Management | X | X | |
| Referral Generation | X | X | |
| Not-in-Person Communications (newsletters, etc.) | X | X | X |

professional decisions and is developing to be a professional while the operations staff is working in a support role and is not expected to pursue a professional career. Needless to say, some of the operations staff may have interest in becoming service advisors and move to that position but that is a change of career tracks rather than career progression.

To help employees develop faster, I am always a proponent of pushing the envelope and allowing (even encouraging) the service advisors to take on a lot of independent responsibility and initiative. The more they stretch their comfort zone, the faster they will learn and the faster they will develop into lead advisors. Of course, there needs to be a good quality control process that ensures that the client's needs do not become "collateral damage" in this learning process.

## Service Advisors and Client Relationships

The service advisors are going to be focused on servicing existing client relationships and therefore, unsurprisingly, they need to know all the clients and then need to quickly absorb all the relevant information regarding the clients' plans, portfolios, and accounts. To achieve this, there is no better method than to bring the advisor into every client meeting and conference call.

For some reason advisors shy away from bringing their service colleagues into a meeting—there is almost certain jealousy if another professional is in the room with the client. That tendency, however, is very counterproductive—the service professionals will have a hard time doing their job without knowledge of the client and exposure to the client. There will certainly be some distraction in the meetings created by the introduction, but that should be a welcome distraction. There is also some risk that the new professional will commit some mistakes (in fact, it is guaranteed that they will), but such risk should be manageable. After all, when a team drafts a quarterback they know for a fact that someday soon he will throw his first interception.

The involvement in meetings and calls should not be just limited to sitting and listening. This does not create many training opportunities and does not establish the role of advisor with the client. In my native Bulgaria they say that if you could learn just by watching then cats would be the best cooks as they spend all their time in the kitchen. Ideally, service advisors are introduced to the client with a clear description of their responsibilities in the firm and in this specific meeting. They should also be assigned a role that will give them a chance to interact with the client and establish their own credibility. Some examples include the following:

- Maintain all notes from the meeting and follow up on execution of the decisions.
- Present a specific analysis as part of the meeting—for example, the performance of an asset class used in the portfolio and how it fits with the strategy.
- Be a specialist in a certain area—for example, "John has great training in financial planning."
- Be responsible for a project—for example, the collection of tax basis data for a portfolio that is about to transfer.

In the process of assigning the service advisor a role in the meetings, the best thing advisors can do is to promote the skills and talent of their new colleague. If you are uncertain and nervous about your colleague, clients will sense that and will be hesitant to work with that person. If, on the other hand, you promote the abilities and training of the professional, clients will be excited to work with them and to take advantage of their skills.

Frequently, advisors think of service advisors as the people who will take over "the small clients." The logic is that if the service advisors tackle the smaller relationships, then the senior advisor can focus on the best clients of the firm. In addition, the risk is lower if something goes wrong in the client relationship. Finally the lead advisor frequently does not enjoy the basic type of work associated with small clients and is happy to delegate it. This logic is often promoted in practice management workshops. However, I am of the strong opinion that this logic is flawed.

I believe that only focusing the time of a service advisor on small relationships is demoralizing to the advisor, often teaches bad habits, and limits the experience of the advisor. There is no way to disguise the fact that the service advisor is being focused on the smallest relationships. If that's indeed the policy, then such a policy can be a real cold shower for the advisor's enthusiasm. It is just difficult to make the statement that "I work with the clients no one else wants to" with any level of pride. The sense of achievement will not be there and often the result is worse rather than better service to the clients targeted. This is also not fair to the clients, they become a "penalty box" rather than as important part of the firm.

What is more, the scope of issues and the types of analysis that the service advisor will be exposed to will be more basic than if they were to work with larger client relationships. The limited complexity creates limited experience, which may mean that the service advisor will be poorly prepared to handle larger relationships later. In fact, the smaller relationships often teach bad habits that can be tolerable in less complex portfolios and plans but may be very problematic with larger relationships.

Most of all, relegating service advisors only to small clients misses the opportunity to leverage the relationships that best lend themselves to it— the large ones. Large and complex projects provide a great training ground and experience as well as afford the budget for teaching and training. Chess coaches say that you learn the most by playing against better players—the higher expectations and standards become a habit and accelerate the exposure to advanced problems. My advice is to provide the service advisors with a mix of smaller relationships that they can "own" and larger relationships where they play the "second chair" role and participate in more complex analysis and decision making.

## From Support to Relationship Management

At some point in their work with a client, service advisors should start not only supporting the lead advisor in their work but also to work as the relationships manager. Assuming the relationship manager role means that clients start to primarily reach to the service advisor for help and are comfortable working directly with the service advisor. That does not mean that they no longer expect to see the lead advisor, but rather that they are comfortable with the lead advisor being in more of a quality control role.

The test for being the relationship manager of a client can be as follows:

- The advisor conducts most (but not all) regularly scheduled meetings with the client independently.
- The client reaches primarily to the advisor when they call.
- The client appears comfortable bringing up new plans or changes in their plan to the advisor and expects the advisor to change the service accordingly.
- The client discusses their satisfaction with the firm with the advisor and is comfortable making comments—complimentary and critical.
- The client reaches out to the advisor when they need additional resources or changes in the service.

The relationship management can be used as a career milestone and a firm could (should) track the clients a professional is managing. The relationship management responsibility can be tied to career goals and promotions as well as to bonus plans. The amount of assets or business that an advisor is a relationship manager for can be a part of a very good incentive compensation formula. It can also be one of the factors that contribute to good partnership criteria down the road.

## From Relationship Management to Ownership of the Client

Once the advisor has become the relationship manager for some clients, the advisor should also start to assume ownership of those clients. This statement usually scares advisors—somebody else taking over ownership of their clients. As scary as that can be, that's a good thing! It should be understood by this point that all clients belong to the firm and that "ownership" really indicates being the lead advisor on the relationship and having the ultimate responsibility for client retention and growth in the relationship.

The transition of ownership of the client means that the owner or lead advisor no longer needs to be part of the client relationship or service and can dedicate his or her time to other relationships. The characteristics of client relationship ownership are the following:

- The advisor conducts all meetings with the client, including important changes to the strategy and new portfolio decisions.
- The client seeks out the advisor and no other senior professionals for advice.
- The advisor has successfully brought new assets or services into the relationship.
- The advisor can delegate a portion of the work to other professionals and the client accepts that process—that is, the circle of leverage starts all over again.

As with the relationship manager role, the owner role should be tied to career plans, including bonuses and perhaps criteria for partner admission.

## The Hiring Process

The key to building an ensemble practice through leverage is identifying the right employees to add to your firm. Most of the struggles, difficulties, and disappointments that many advisors have experienced when working with "junior advisors" can be attributed to a poor fit between the candidate and the position rather than to some inherent problem in working with service advisors. In order to be successful in making this key hire, advisors have to be thoughtful and systematic in their approach to hiring rather than opportunistically grab the first candidate they come across. The keys to making a good hire are the following:

1. **Don't make it a one-horse race—advertise the position**. Too often firms tend to reach out and bring on board someone they know as soon as they start the discussion of hiring an employee advisor. That person may or may not be a fit for the position (more often not), and his or her poor fit with the position may sabotage the whole plan. Rather than thinking about whether a person is a good candidate for a position and hiring the first good candidate, firms need to think about who is the *best candidate* and treat the position as a prized resource that should be given to the best applicant. In order to do that, you will need to advertise the position and gather information on many applicants. As a rule of thumb, when we fill a position in my firm (The Ensemble Practice LLC) we seek to have at

least 10 qualified candidates who submit a resume before we are ready to begin interviewing. If we don't have 10, we need to advertise more.

There are many places to advertise a position that are effective, and you should utilize multiple services. That said, we have found that we get the best results from the following:

- The FPA job posting service—a great resource for service advisor hiring.
- Local FPA chapters—very focused posting but varies from state to state.
- CareerBuilder.com—creates wide exposure of the ad to many candidates.
- LinkedIn and similar professional networks.

Needless to say, some of the best candidates will come from referrals—from wholesalers, from colleagues and from other firms in the area. Reaching out to all of those relationships and sending them a copy of the job ad is highly recommended. The candidates that come from such a referral are likely of high quality but should go through the same process as all other candidates.

2. **Develop a job description.** It is very difficult to match somebody to a position that you have not yet described. The job description should be developed before you write the ad for the position and should include the job responsibilities, the position's place in the organization, including reporting, key measures of success for the position, required skills and knowledge, required experience, and finally desirable (but not required) qualifications. Ideally you will also determine the range of compensation for the position and the factors that will drive the decision to move a person within the range. This last part of the document does not need to be made immediately available to candidates or be part of the ad but will certainly help compensation decisions later.

3. **Have a process and follow it.** The recruiting decision should be the result of a carefully thought out process rather than a "gut reaction" after a few interviews. Ideally the process combines:

   **a.** Initial screening of the resumes submitted (require a resume from all candidates—even those coming from referral) for fit with the job description (see above).

   **b.** A first-round interview that explores the candidates past experience, their career goals, their proficiency in professional topics, communication style and skills, and so on.

   **c.** Samples of prior work or short case developed as a test of knowledge and application to real-life situations—a very good idea.

   **d.** Background check—a must.
   **e.** Job matching test for communication and thinking style—not a must but very revealing.
   **f.** A second-round interview focused on the areas of concern identified by tests, further honing in on the goals of the individual, his or her thinking style, ability to work in a team, and so on.

   My strong recommendation is that you never short-cut the process regardless of how well you feel about a candidate. It is also never a good idea to yield to pressure such as "I have another offer, which I have to accept by Monday." In my personal experience, every time we have done that we have regretted the decision.

4. **Make an offer.** We will discuss compensation at length in Chapter 6, but there are a few points that we need to make here with regard to making offers:

   **a.** Make a written official offer—verbal offers are ripe with opportunity for misunderstanding.
   **b.** Incorporate the right nonsolicitation language in the offer—you should work with your attorneys to make sure that there is appropriate language covering nonsolicitation of clients in the event the employee leaves.
   **c.** Describe accurately your:
      i. Bonus plans.
      ii. Benefits packages.
      iii. Vacation and time-off policies.

   **d.** Don't haggle—generally, you don't want to create the impression that the prospective employee can negotiate salary or compensation. One of the purposes of a written offer is to create that sense of finality to the offer. That said, you do want to stay open to hearing the thoughts of the candidate on the offer. If there are valid, well-argued reasons for modifying the offer, you should hear those and perhaps incorporate them in a revised offer.
   **e.** Don't custom compensate—A common experience for advisors when hiring is to learn that their best candidates have a history of higher compensation in their current job. In general, we recommend that our clients not violate their compensation philosophy and their pay ranges for a candidate. As long as you have the confidence that your compensation ranges are competitive and fair, the history of a candidate is irrelevant. If they were happy with their current job, they would not be applying for this one, so there must be factors driving them to seek a change. Further, candidates tend to exaggerate their

pay—consciously or unconsciously. They tend to combine their projected salary for next year, their highest bonus, and the value of their benefits into a single number. A statement such as "I was paid $90,000" often means "I had a salary of $60,000 but it would have been $65,000 next year, I expect a bonus of $10,000 this year, and my benefits plus 401(k) match must be around $15,000."

5. **Hire family, friends, and clients.** Many advisors work with their sons and daughters. Many hire family, friends, or family and friends of clients. There is nothing wrong with that decision as long as you are prepared to treat your family and friends exactly the same way you treat your employees. You must be willing to be just as critical or praising and just as strict or lenient as you are toward any other employee. Realistically, most people can't do that. Most advisors end up overindulging their family and are afraid to ask them to improve their performance. Others are too critical of their children and kill their enthusiasm. What is more, other employees find it hard and awkward to work with the family. For that combination of reasons, I am not a fan at all of hiring family. The only exception is family members who have established their career in another firm and are joining with a well-defined experience and skill set.

## The Selling Question

Most advisors who hire a service advisor for the first time can't resist the temptation to ask themselves, "Can we get this person to sell, and how can we get them to sell more?" The question is understandable—after all, having someone to contribute to the top line will make the position much more affordable and will also alleviate the pressure from the owner. However, we have to remember that the goal of this position is leverage, not sales. What is more, if relatively inexperienced advisors can develop any business, it is usually the wrong business. They tend to generate small accounts with clients that do not always fit the target profile of the business.

We also have to be realistic—of all the responsibilities discussed in Table 3.1, from marketing to servicing clients, to managing relationships, generating leads is the scarcest skill and requires the most experience. In fact, my experience has been that a professional needs 10 to 12 years of quality experience in a market before he or she can become an effective business developer. In other words, it will be a long time before a person hired as a service advisor and who has four or five years of experience can help you develop new business. That said, their training should begin now.

The business development training should consist of the following:

- Training to recognize opportunities—The first training for business development should be the ability to recognize opportunities with existing clients. Every professional in the firm should be expected to look for indicators that clients may need additional services. If professionals are not comfortable proposing additional services to clients they already know well, they will never be comfortable presenting to strangers. The recognition of opportunities is not always automatic, though—the firm may need to train service advisors for signs of additional needs as well as giving them examples of situations that led to additional services.
- Training in presenting to clients—The best way to learn to hold successful business development meetings is to observe good meetings. A great way of training advisors to sell is to simply bring them to your sales meetings. They will have a chance to see you at work as well as to play a role in those meetings. It's like cooking a dish you have never tasted yourself—it is very difficult to do. It is much easier to cook something you have seen your mom prepare many times.
- Understanding the sales process—Less experienced professionals need a sales process to be successful. Too often they tend to think of business development as a single meeting or event while the reality is that it is often a sequence of communications leading to a client decision. The more structured the sequence, the easier it is for less experienced people to execute it. Inexperienced advisors cannot conceptualize a process all on their own, though; they need help in putting the steps together, and they need to observe how the process works.
- Exposure to referral sources—One of the best ways to plant the seeds of future business development is to introduce your younger professionals to your referral sources. Referral source relationships do not always transfer easily; they are often more personal than institutional (i.e., John Taxovich, the partner of the local CPA firm, works with you personally because you know each other rather than the two firms having a relationship). Still, an introduction will provide exposure to the service professionals that may become productive or at least may prompt the other professional to introduce their associates to your firm. In the beginning of my career, one of the partners in Moss Adams introduced me to a couple of partners in a large local law firm. It's not that the senior law firm partners ever made any referral to me, but they in turn introduced me to a couple of their associate attorneys who later became good professional relationships.

- Developing presence and reputation—Developing a foundation of referral sources and market presence that can create referrals is a process that takes years to fruition and should begin early in a person's career. Service advisors should start being active in community organizations, networking groups, and professional organizations early in their career. This allows them to build relationships with future sources of referral without the pressure of immediate results. They can take their time to get to know their peers at the local accounting and law firm, meet the future business leaders, and create a presence in local organizations without having to promote their own agenda. Instead they can build connections and visibility, which later will naturally give them business opportunities.

    These early efforts in developing a network will also help service advisors develop good marketing habits. Too often advisors develop careers in an internal environment with no exposure to marketing. It is very difficult for an experienced advisor with a high position and compensation to humble themselves to market and network. Not marketing early in a career also misses the opportunity to get to know the future leaders and stars of local businesses before they become the center of everyone's attention. I still remember eating $3 nachos with the CEO of one of the largest wealth management firms in the country when we were both in our 20s. It will be impossible to establish the same relationship later in our careers—if nothing else, now that we are older, everyone is on a diet.

In other words, less experienced advisors may not be able to contribute immediately to the top line, but if they develop the right habits and are consistently encouraged to engage in marketing, the day will come when you will not be the only business developer in the firm.

## The Equity Question

When hiring a service advisor, owners of advisory firms are very likely to encounter the question of whether or not the firm offers equity opportunities to advisors. Just as a young attorney or CPA joining a firm expects some day to become a partner in that same firm, it has very much become the expectation in the advisory industry that young professionals will be able to earn the right to join the partner group. The "equity question" is not always asked during the interview process and may not even come up in an open dialogue for the first couple of years, but as an owner you can be assured that it is in the back of every candidate's mind and sooner or later you will have to deal with it. As always, my preference is to be open about your position and to create the right expectations from the beginning.

The worst mistake you can make with the equity question is to promise something you are not prepared to deliver. Of all possible ways of addressing the desire of every advisor to someday become an owner is to explicitly or implicitly lead him or her to expect to become a partner some day when you really don't want to or don't plan to have partners. Therefore the first step toward addressing the equity question is to ask yourself—am I open some day to having a partner? Can I share decision-making power, responsibility, and income with another person? Will I be comfortable with accepting the decisions of another person and being bound by the consequences of those decisions? Unless you can answer such questions positively, it is best not to create expectations with advisors.

If you are not sure if you will ever want to have a partner but you are open to the idea, good possible answers can be in the form of "*As the firm grows and evolves there may come a time when adding a partner becomes possible. However, at present I don't have plans to offer equity to any professional in the firm. As the firm changes this may change as well, but I can't make any promises for the future. Instead, we rely on a combination of great compensation, good training, and a caring work environment to reward and grow the career of our professionals.*"

Answers that are likely to get you in trouble are usually in the form of veiled promises such as "*We are a small firm and I haven't really had a chance to think about this much—it's just too early. I am sure, though, that if you start making a contribution to the firm we can figure something out.*"

It is my belief that while synthetic equity such as options, phantom stock, and profits interest have their role in the compensation and equity structure of a firm (usually a very large firm), that's not what professionals have in mind when they inquire about equity opportunity. If you allude to the possibility of partnership or equity in the early conversations with a professional, you will find that he or she is likely to be disappointed by phantom stock or other synthetic vehicles.

On the other hand, you should not be too specific answering the question, unless you really mean to be very specific. For example, a statement such as "*When we reach $2 million in revenue you will have equity in the firm,*" is very specific and should not be made unless this is exactly your intention. Note that this statement also excludes any other important factors in the decision such as the performance of the employee, their contribution to business development, their responsibilities, and so forth that should be part of the decision.

Finally, if you plan to offer partnership opportunities in the future and you feel you can discuss the opportunity with employees, it is very constructive to outline the general process—the general criteria for partnership consideration, the overall process for buying into the firm, and the general growth expectations for the firm. For example, "*To consider someone as a future partner we look at their contribution to the business, their level of professional expertise, their ability to develop new business, and their ability to manage and supervise employees. We give individuals who excel in each of those areas the chance to buy into the equity of the firm and become partners, and we make that decision also based on the growth of the firm—we can only add new partners if the firm is growing in revenues and profits.*"

Equity opportunities can be a fantastic motivator and can be the crowning achievement of the first stage of a professional career, but they should be used very carefully and sparingly. Speaking about equity before you are ready with your decision can be detrimental and set up problems in the future. At the same time, dodging the question and not providing any clarity is actually worse than just saying "No—we don't do that!"

We will discuss in great detail in Chapter 8 how you can select your future partners and how to structure their deals so that you make this opportunity available only to the best advisors in the firm and without diluting the equity and income of current partners.

## Making the Decision

Adding the first employee advisor to the firm is perhaps the most significant decision you will make as a business owner. It is also one of the most difficult decisions you will make as a business owner—you are focusing a lot of expectations and a lot of resources on a single individual. The return on that investment can be very high, and this is certainly a necessary step toward building an ensemble firm. It is also true, though, that there is a significant chance that the first employee advisor you hire may not be the star performer that will help you grow the firm to new highs. Unfortunately you have to accept that there is a risk that you will hire the wrong person for the job, or that a star performer will be lured away by another firm, or that life will take them somewhere else and they will change careers or cities. When you embark on the journey of hiring professionals and building a firm, you have to accept the risk that the first path you take will be a dead end. If that happens you just have to start all over again and take everything you learn and apply it to the next hire. In 1980 a lady by the name of Marla Wood left a small software company in the Seattle area called Microsoft.[4] She was quite unhappy when she left. She was hired to be an assistant/manager and work with one of the founders—Bill Gates—but unfortunately that relationship did not work out well. Her "replacement" was a gentleman by the name of Steve Ballmer who dropped out of the Stanford Graduate School of Business to become the first business manager of the company. Today Ballmer is the CEO of Microsoft.

## Notes

1. According to research firm Cerulli and Associates. Helen Kearny, "Ranks of US financial advisers shrinking," Reuters, August 11, 2010.
2. CFP Certification Exam Statistics published by CFP Board of Standards, www.cfp.net/media/survey.asp?id=9#2.
3. "2003 FPA Staffing and Compensation Survey," Moss Adams LLP.
4. "When Microsoft was local—how its first 11 employees fared," *The Albuquerque Tribune*, April 12, 2000.

# CHAPTER 4

# Merging Together

The first question advisors ask when they consider a merger is "How do we structure the deal?" In reality this should be the last matter on the table. Instead, the first question should be "Why are we doing this?" A merger has a dramatic impact on both practices involved, and that impact will be felt for as long as you are an owner in the firm. The merger will change your practice through the decisions you make together with your partners, the culture and interactions in the office, the relationship with employees you manage together, and the clients who meet with you and your partners. The effect of the deal structure, on the other hand, will only be felt when you chose to sell the firm or retire. This is why I believe it is important to start with a strong understanding of why you are considering the merger, what you expect of your future partners, how you will interact with them, and what will be the outcome for the clients. Only if there is an agreement on strategy and responsibilities, can you proceed with discussions of revenues, profits and income before you finally arrive at the topic of equity and valuations.

I cannot possibly emphasize enough the importance of carefully choosing your merger partners and thinking and engaging in an honest dialogue with your merger candidates. The inevitable parallel here is to compare a merger to a marriage—it is this delicate tangle of personalities, contributions, history, daily behavior, and the sense of building something together. This may sound like an exaggeration but when I mentioned this parallel in a conversation with a client one time, he told me, "No kidding, it is like a marriage, except for the last 25 years I have had the same partner but three different wives." That said, the track record of mergers is much worse than marriages—if only 50 percent of marriages survive, in my estimate, less than a third of the partnerships that are formed will survive for more than five years.

The best possible mergers are those where both advisors can quickly see how the two practices will complement each other and how the combination will enhance the ability of both firms to deliver services to their clients and compete better in the marketplace. What is more, there should be a strong mutual respect between the practitioners and a genuine belief that the other person is someone whom you can trust. As long as those two factors are in place—sense of purpose and mutual respect—everything else can be adjusted, negotiated, accommodated, and redesigned. There is no future in any merger discussion, however, if you do not feel that the other practice can enhance yours and that you do not value and respect the other professional or professionals.

With the risk of "kicking a dead horse"—ask yourself if you would trust the other person to manage your spouse's financial affairs if something were to happen to you. If the answer is not a firm "Yes," I would be skeptical about the future of the merger. If you simply do not know the person well, that's a different problem that can easily be solved—simply take the time to get to know him or her better. Never enter into a merger with someone whom you do not trust and respect and who does not trust and respect you back. To quote my mentor Ed Drosdick again, "No one can increase the quality of your life as much as a good partner can; then again, no one can make you as miserable as your partner." Proceed with caution.

My advice to clients who are contemplating mergers is that they should spend a lot of time in discussion and getting to know each other, patiently collecting information about each other's business as well as understanding each other as professionals and people. Most successful discussions take anywhere from six months to two years so patience is necessary. It is not unusual to see professionals "bouncing back and forth" the idea of a merger for years before entering into a specific discussion of how to accomplish the deal. Take your time.

Before embarking on the mechanics of a merger process I would also like to leave behind some of the notions that advisors may have developed through reading about acquisitions in the advisory business. There are many acquisition deals publicized but advisors should realize there is a tremendous difference between the deals done by consolidators, banks, and broker-dealers and a merger between two advisory firms. Deals are transactions, mergers are relationships. Deals tend to emphasize factors such as valuations, covenants, cash flows, and multiples. Successful mergers start with relationship, decision making, accountability, and shared values. I am not usually the one to take the soft and squishy side over a good corporate finance spreadsheet,[1] but putting the spreadsheets in front of the people in this case would be like putting the cart in front of the horses and then telling the horses that they are now demoted and will have to report to the executive vice president of cart management.

I advise clients who are embarking on a merger discussion to roughly break the process into six steps, listed below. We will discuss each step in this chapter and some of them deserve an entire chapter of their own (namely, strategy and compensation). Each step should take at least one, possibly several meetings, and there is a lot of merit in keeping personal and shared notes throughout this discussion so that you can continuously refer back to questions you have already considered together.

1. **The big idea—discussion of your shared strategy**—What are the reasons you are combining you firms? How will the combination make you more successful and competitive? Who are you competing with? Who will be your target clients? What services will you provide? What will be your goals for the next five years? What do you envision the firm will look like five years from now? What do you see happening beyond the next five years?

2. **Discussion of your personal goals**—What motivates you as an individual? What business values do you hold? What do you enjoy and hate doing? What do you see as your strengths? What culture are you looking to create? What are your goals personally? What is the income you draw from the business? What is the income you desire?

3. **Sharing and discussion of data**—At this step, share financials and payroll data as well as organizational charts and job descriptions. In addition, research client data and statistics and pricing of services for the other practice. When you have the information, study it carefully and ask each other clarifying questions

4. **Business planning**—Assuming you are still interested in the merger, discuss what the combined organization will look like. You should also create a combined organization chart and discuss office locations and logistics, responsibilities of each partner, and the mechanics of client service. Consider who will develop new business and what kind of business. Spend some time on what systems will survive the merger and what the combined financials will look like. Finally, define what the milestones for combining the firms will be.

5. **Partnership structure**—What will be your responsibilities as partners? Who will get paid and how? Will you have profit centers or will you operate a combined profit and loss (P&L)? What will be your titles? How will you make decisions? How will you use and distribute/contribute

capital? What are the current liabilities of each firm? How will you deal with those liabilities? What are the future risks and how will you deal with them? Will there be a buy/sell agreement?

6. **Deal**—The final step is to consider the valuations or formulas for combining the practices and any legal provisions to your agreement.

## Your Shared Strategy

We will devote an entire chapter to discussing the strategy of ensemble firms in Chapter 9, but we need to outline some of the strategies that can be complementary and that will lead to successful mergers. It has been my experience that mergers succeed when the underlying reason is one of the following:

- A combination of complementary skills and resources—for example, a strong investment management firm and a good financial planning firm.
- Desire to reach critical mass with respect to one or more valuable resources— be a bigger employer, be a bigger presence in a valuable market, be able to afford a research department, and so on.
- Genuine desire to practice in a collegiate atmosphere—believe it or not, just sharing the experience is a good reason to merge as long as it is shared.
- Create a succession and continuity plan for the owners either directly (one partner will be the successor) or by together hiring the next generation.

There are many poor reasons for a merger, of course, and the most prominent among those are reading a book about how the future belongs to ensembles, combining to sell to an acquirer together for a higher multiple, "busting out of jail together"—that is, leaving a broker-dealer together, collective bargaining—such as combining practices for a bigger recruiting bonus—access to the clients of the other firm (if not reciprocal), and so on.

Usually, it's a good exercise to try to visualize the combined firm after the transition is complete and ask yourself: "What will the firm look like?" If you were to describe this firm to a prospective client, would they find it compelling? Why? What would be the strengths of the new firm[2] and what would be the weaknesses? Test the new value proposition with colleagues and perhaps even trusted clients. Most of all, look for signs that the competitive advantages you are focusing on are real rather than perceived. For example, it is a very valid reason to try to appear as a larger firm to clients and referral sources. The presence of your partners may convey stability, continuity, and depth. On the other hand, be realistic—will going from a three-person firm to a five-person firm suddenly change the perception of your firm dramatically?

Finally, there should be agreement and excitement over the strategy. Both parties to a merger should share the view that indeed an advantage will be created and that such advantage can be captured. The opportunity should also be something you are interested in personally and excited about. Reluctant mergers have the same feeling to them as prearranged marriages. I often see professionals who are going through a merger because they are convinced that they "have to" improve something about their practice—for example, create succession or gain access to a good planning department. That mechanical improvement may work in large public corporations, but it can kill the enthusiasm of the entrepreneur-advisor, and a practice with an unenthusiastic owner is like a car without gas.

Entering into a merger because you feel it is "the right thing to do" will give you the exact same odds as smokers trying to quit because they "have to." Trust me, as I was a smoker for almost 20 years. Unless you come to a deep conviction that you "want" to quit, rather than "have to," you are bound to fail because your entire body will be screaming "Don't you wish you could have another cigarette!" I have seen many professionals who croon over the "good old days" before the merger—don't join them. If you are not convinced you want to enter into an ensemble firm and have a partner—take your time and determine the reasons why you would want to do it.

## Your Shared Values

A good merger is grounded in good partner communications and relationship. The relationship should be one of respect and trust. Unless you trust each other, it will be impossible to make decisions; you will always be second-guessing each other. Unless you trust each other, it will also be impossible to lead people together—you will be like quarrelling parents who are giving their children conflicting messages. Finally, unless you trust each other, you will never be able to come to an agreement on how to share income and compensation. Trust and respect go hand in hand-to trust each other you have to respect each other.

I really have no formal training in the area of human relationships and especially partnerships, but I have had some years of personal experience in various partnerships and interactions with different partners. From my experience, I can tell you that it is not important at all for the partners' personalities to be carbon copies of eachother. In fact, too much of the same personality type may be more destructive than constructive. A good partnership also does not mean that one partner has to submit his or her ego to the other and follow some sort of a wolf-pack alpha-beta model. I have been very fortunate to have had wonderful partners in my entire career, and I assure you that our personalities were nothing alike. Neither were our backgrounds or our life experiences. Many traits were shared but just as many were vastly different. I can also tell you that I along with every single one of my partners have as big an ego as you can fit in an Egyptian pyramid, and still we had no trouble functioning together and making decisions together. I believe the reason behind that experience was trust—we trusted each other and respected each other and that allowed everything else to fall in place.

How do you get to trust and respect someone? How can you establish that in a due diligence process? To be honest, I am not sure. I sort of grew up with one of my partners. Rebecca Pomering, who is a well-known expert, CEO, and compensation guru in the advisor industry, and I started working together when we were each 24 or 25 years old. By the time we became business partners we had years and years of history of working together through times thick and thin. Mark Tibergien, who more or less invented practice management in the advisory industry, was another partner of mine.[3] He was my mentor and teacher and as a result trusting him was an instinct rather than a conscious process. This is why the internal process of partners who create a practice together tends to be more reliable and more lasting. Unfortunately it is very slow.

Stuart Silverman, CEO and founder of Fusion, and my partner in that business, on the other hand, was a partner I sort of "merged" with. With Stuart I had to get to know and understand him before we could establish that same level of trust and respect for each other. That process was more difficult than starting in business together and not without friction but no less successful.

How can you get to know a person to the point that you trust them? I would really start by asking them questions—what would they do? How would they do it? Why are they doing this or that? I would also try to observe them in variety of situations—how do they interact with their clients? With their prospects? How do they treat their employees?

It is always a good idea to get to know the other person's family—not because you will be seeing each other at every summer picnic and holiday party but because the way they interact with their family and the way they think about their family will probably tell you a lot about the person they are. Last but not least, I would not be shy about asking people who might know them for their impressions. Subject to confidentiality of course, you can gather information on the other party from the local chapters of professional associations, shared referral sources, and perhaps even shared acquaintances. The world is a surprisingly small place.

## The Data

When you are confident that you have a strategic fit with the other practice and you believe that you can work well with the owner(s) of the other firm, it will be time to gather some data. At this point you should have a confidentiality (nondisclosure) agreement with the other party and have the peace of mind that the data exchanged will not be misused. If you are not certain of that—do not proceed.

The data gathering typically covers five areas—the clients, the investments, the people, the operations, and the financials. The following list can be useful, but it is by no means complete or suitable for every single transaction:

Clients—Remember that your firm and the other firm each have their own client privacy policies, which you have to follow. Do not disclose information your policy does not allow you to disclose. This may include the fact that a person is a client. If you have a broker-dealer (BD), your BD may have his or her own privacy policy that you have to comply with. Subject to those restrictions, a list of clients' accounts with no names but showing account balances will give you a good sense of the client base. Ideally you can also see a breakdown by the occupation of the clients, age, and other important demographic criteria. A breakdown of the tenure of clients with the firm (length of the relationship) will give you a sense of the continuity. In some cases it might be telling to see the city or zip code breakdown of the clients if the geography of the area is important— some cities are more homogenous but others are divided in more self-contained communities. Finally, a list of clients who joined the firm in the last two years and the clients who left can give you a sense of the business development process and retention in the firm.

Investments—It will be great to see all model portfolios used (if applicable), investment proposals, and investment policy statements for the other firms. A breakdown of the asset flows into new assets from new clients, new assets from existing clients, performance, distributions, and lost clients is also very telling.

**People**—Here you should ask for a complete roster of the firm, together with positions, compensation history (including bonuses), and job description. It is also useful to go through the profile of each person with your merger partner—how long have they been with the firm? What are they like? How are they performing? Who's due for promotion?

**Operations**—As with clients, some of the information may belong to a third party, so you may need to modify your request. You should understand the primary systems used—performance reporting, billing, rebalancing, CRM, e-mail, paperless office, financial planning, and others. You also want to get a good picture of the level of satisfaction with each system and the future plans for change, if any. The custodian and/or broker-dealer will play a decisive role in this process so they should be well understood—payouts, ticket charges, platform fees, break-points, reputation and performance, flexibility to work with other custodians and BDs, and so on.

**Financials**—This is probably the first folder you will open and the curiosity is justified. After all, every management decision sooner or later leaves its mark on the financials statement. Here you should request three years of financial statements (P&L and balance sheet) as well as the last year to date fiscal year (e.g., year to date as of October 2013). If there are any other significant contracts that impact the balance sheet, you would probably want to at least discuss them if not obtain a copy. Those may include loans to shareholders or employees, lease agreements, stock option or similar plans, and the like.

We will discuss in Chapter 11 the process of analyzing the data, but in short, you will be looking for the quality of the client relationships, the ability to add new clients and retain existing ones, investment decisions that are consistent with your philosophy, and business operations that are compatible with yours. In the financials we will look for profitability, cash flow, stability and consistency, and any land mines that may sink an otherwise healthy ship (dependence on one large client, significant future liability, overdrawing capital, etc.).

Once you obtain the data, you should schedule a sequence of meetings to discuss it and answer clarifying questions. A common mistake is to jump to conclusions and start asking the other party loaded questions—questions that make more of a statement than ask for information. For example, "Have you noticed the quality of your client base is worse than mine?" Take the time to be patient here and not to rush to conclusions before you have all the information. The way you gather information will certainly impact the tone of all future discussions.

## The Business Plan

"The devil is always in the details," and the actual implementation of the merger strategy is often the first test of the future ensemble partnership. Every area of the business will be impacted by the merger, and therefore you will need to examine the entire business plan for the firm. Generally, the discussion should center on the following topics:

- **Business transition**—The merger may require a number of structural changes such as change of broker-dealers or custodians. This generates a complex set of issues that have been well documented in many articles and white papers. Still, I would encourage you to focus on the long-term future of the firm rather than the short-term transition cost or hassle.
- **Physical space**—Many advisors own the building they rent, and as a result the issue of physical space may become a surprising stumbling block. Ideally, the two practices share an office (critical for integration), and the choice of offices is not driven by the ownership of buildings and commute times (within reason).
- **Compliance**—There might be a number of regulatory filings necessary in order to effect the merger, especially if both firms have their own RIA. It is also worth examining the processes of both firms and appointing a new combined chief compliance officer who will select the prevailing new procedures.
- **Technology and operations**—Chances are that the two practices use different systems for their key functions, particularly performance reporting, trading, and customer relationship management (CRM). You will need to examine the systems of both practices, their ability to support the combined firm, and the future needs of the business. This may be a job for one of the leaders in your organization who can rise to the occasion to take ownership of the technology integration. This brings up the important issue of the timing of your disclosure of the pending merger to your employees—an issue discussed at the end of this chapter.

The key with such operational details is to always keep an eye on what is "the horse" and what is "the cart" in the merger—as in "not putting the cart in front of the horse." Details such as choosing a joint office and a joint custodian or broker-dealer should not be driving the deal. Instead, there should be a discussion of what is the best custodian(s) or broker-dealer for the combined organization, rather than "I don't want to be changing custodians." It is amazing how many merger negotiations die because no one wants to change offices—something that should be a relatively minor aspect of the new relationship.

## Partner Roles and Compensation

The issue of partner compensation is discussed in Chapter 6 and trust me, it is a long chapter, but we need to leave some notes within the context of structuring and negotiating the merger. At this point in the discussion you should be convinced that barring setbacks related to valuations and compensation, you will be consummating this agreement. If you are not certain you want to do this deal, it is worth going back a couple of steps before embarking on compensation modeling. Given that a deal is close, you should not be shy about discussing what role you will perform in the new business and how each of the owners will be compensated. Any sensitivity at this point should yield to the need for clarity.

Start with a very specific discussion of responsibilities in the new firm— compensation should really start with what the partners do as a job in the firm and whether it will be compensated on a variable (payout) or fixed (salary) basis. A key question is to what degree partner compensation will depend on the partner's revenue production or be a relatively fixed based on their job worth. Once you determine the base compensation of the partners, you will need to run a quick financial projection for the combined firm, inclusive of the proposed compensation method. Examine the impact of the compensation decision on profitability—how much of the income of the firm is "dropping to the bottom line" and is that more or less than you expected? Think about the addition of an owner "bonus" to compensate for management responsibilities or significant contribution that is missed by the base compensation. You will find further guidance on this topic in the next chapter.

Finally, look at the new compensation method and project realistically the impact on your personal financial plan. Are you making as much as you need to cover your personal expenses? Does this income allow you to meet personal financial goals? You should be very realistic in this projection and not forecast steep growth numbers. If your personal goals are not met, you will need to seriously consider if the merger is still viable. You can't ask a new partner for more compensation because "I need it." At the same time, if the merger reduces your income and you can't afford the reduction, perhaps now is not the best time to be honest with yourself and your potential partners. Look at this situation as if a client had asked you for advice—what would you say?

## The Deal

When you are first entering into a partnership with another advisor, you have a blank canvas on which you can draw your ideal structure. There are no preset expectations and no set ways of thinking. You should use that opportunity wisely and not rush to the easiest outcome (e.g., 50—50). The key questions are "Who is bringing what to the firm and what is the value of that contribution?" Contribution may come in the form of revenue and clients, capital, staff and infrastructure, experience and know-how, among others. Some of the forms of contribution may be easier to value than others, but that should not preclude the question "How much is this worth to the firm?"

In a merger between two practices, my first instinct would be to look at the profit contribution that each practice will be making to the new firm. If the value of the firm is driven by its profitability and cash flow, then bringing profits should be the most valuable kind of contribution. To do that, you will need to:

- Remove all nonrecurring and discretionary expenses from the P&L.
- Adjust for nonrecurring revenue.
- Annualize new relationships that is, those that started during the last fiscal year and do not have a full year of billing.
- Apply any pricing changes that will be effective after the merger, for example, if one of the practices is changing broker-dealers.
- Apply any staffing or other expense changes that will occur as a result of the merger.

The resulting statement (accountants will call that a pro forma statement) will give you an idea of the potential contribution of profits each practice will have in the new firm. It will be hard to argue that if a practice contributes 60 percent of the profitability of the new firm, its owner should not be a 60 percent owner of the combined firm, everything else being equal.

Except, everything else is never equal! Before you finalize such a merger agreement, it's worth also looking at the following:

- What are the rates of growth of each practice? Is one growing faster?
- Is one practice generating more recurring revenue than the other?

- Is there a different level of risk in each practice? For example, one operates like a hedge fund and the other is more "plain vanilla"?
- Is one practice bringing some needed regulatory expertise and registrations —for example, an existing registered investment advisor (RIA) firm?

If the process of preparing a pro forma is not practical or agreeable, then often practices merge based on revenue or assets under management (AUM). The underlying assumption again is that if one practice is bringing 60 percent of the revenue, it most likely is also bringing 60 percent of the profitability. This assumption has to be understood and accepted by both parties. There are many reasons why one practice may be more profitable than the other, but sometimes those are difficult to demonstrate in a negotiation. Assets are an even greater "leap of faith" and imply that the same amount of assets generates the same amount of revenue and therefore the same level of profit. Still, this may be the most practical assumption to negotiate compared to making somewhat arbitrary pro forma adjustments.

Valuations are also a good method for estimating the merger percentages. Both practices can ask a valuation expert to compile an estimate of their report and then the two can calculate the resulting percentages. It is imperative in such situations to use the same exact firm for both practices and to explain to the firm the reason for the valuation so that they can apply the most consistent methodology across both firms. I am also very partial to using valuation firms that specialize in this industry such as FP Transitions and Moss Adams rather than a generic firm.

## Mergers of Not So Equals

Nonreciprocal merger agreements are very difficult to negotiate and complete. Generally, as soon as one side brings up the argument that it is supplying all the infrastructure, know-how, and regulatory experience and therefore should be valued higher on a dollar for dollar basis, the negotiation tends to fall apart. It's a bit like saying "My kids are smarter than yours." It is never a good way to make friends. Still, the argument is often made by larger companies that merge breakaway advisors into an existing firm.

While the logic of the argument is very strong, it emotionally difficult to accept and for practical purposes it may be very difficult to quantify the premium that should be associated with the greater size. Larger firms tend to overvalue the "infrastructure" While smaller firms tend to underestimate its importance. That's where the negotiations tend to abruptly end.

A similar problem occurs when one side claims a "size premium," arguing that since it is larger it will command a higher multiple in the market if it were sold. This again is a good theoretical argument that never works in practice. While size premiums are very much a reality in the mergers and acquisitions (M&A) market, there is really not that much of a difference between how a $1 million firm and a $2 million firm are valued. In summary, if you are negotiating from the position of being the larger firm, you have to be very careful with how you price the premiums you are asking for or you risk losing the deal quickly. If you are the smaller firm, you should consider carefully the value of the larger firm's infrastructure.

That said, many firms merge into much bigger ones as a way of accessing resources. It is important to realize in such deals that the bigger firm likely has very specific ideas about the deal structure, and as the smaller firm your negotiating power will be very limited. In such cases I would advise that you spend a lot of time educating yourself about their partner compensation process and really emphasize the income (as opposed to equity) part of the deal. Realistically, your equity will be in a minority position and with severe restrictions on how you can sell it and to whom. The income is really the primary motivator for such deals, and therefore you should focus the negotiations on that component of the deal.

## The Deals after the Deal

The first equity deal is rarely the last—chances are that the new ensemble firm will add more partners in the future, may buy out some partners, or change the equity percentages. I believe it is healthy for every partnership to spend some time every year discussing the current equity arrangement and any anticipated changes. Some of the reasons why you may want to adjust the ownership include the following:

- Disconnect between equity and contribution.
- A partner wants to "slow down."
- A new partner is about to be admitted.
- A partner wants to retire in the next five years.

It is impossible to anticipate every future situation, and therefore it is difficult to plan for each of these events in the operating agreement. Some firms try to set rules for how an internal "market" for the equity of the firm will operate, including setting formulas for valuation and a window for transactions. This tends to be a feature of very large partnerships and is not very practical for smaller firms since there is usually no "trading" at the window. It is much more important to maintain an agreement that as such circumstances arise, the partners will address them in a fair and thoughtful manner. Setting valuation parameters within the operating agreement is a good idea for buy-sell agreements but may not be the best way of dealing with the situations just listed.

## Owner Rights

I hear the declaration "I will never be a minority owner" so often that it is surprising that any mergers ever occur. My response is usually that I have personally never been a majority owner in any business (my house, included for that matter), so I really don't understand what the fuss is about. Most of the time I find that the issues that potential minority owners are concerned with can effectively be dealt with through a well-crafted operating agreement that gives the minority owners some specific protection. This agreement should be discussed with your attorney, and you may want to consider obtaining the following rights as a minority owner by requiring a supermajority vote or simply having the right to veto some of the decisions:

- Sale of the business—This goes without saying or explanation.
- Addition of another owner to the business—This is a critical decision and should only be made unanimously. It is a very bad step for a partnership if it adds a partner that is not approved by all.
- Issuing of new shares—Needless to say, this can lead to dilution of the existing owners. Even if antidilution rights are in place, you may find that you need to purchase new shares to exercise those when you do not have enough capital.
- Capital calls—A capital call, the request to put new money into the business or lose part or all of your ownership, is a very unpleasant occurrence and can wreak havoc on the finances of a new owner. Unfortunately, those are sometimes inevitable. Still, having the right to block those may give you the chance to make sure that all other options are exhausted.
- Executive compensation—As we discussed above, owner compensation decisions can drastically change the profitability of the business.
- Dividend distributions—This may be impossible to do (especially in an S corporation), but usually younger owners prefer more frequent distributions while the older owners generally tend to be more conservative

with the capital. These issues are best solved in a discussion, but consider what kind of vote is necessary in order to affect a distribution.

- Hiring of executives—Some key employees, even if they are not owners, can significantly alter the profitability and the management decision making of the business and may be of special interest to the minority owners.
- Change of broker-dealer or custodian —The change of broker-dealers (if applicable) may change completely the "ownership" of client relationships and the client contract and is a very important decision to consider in the voting rights.

This is by no means a complete list, and with your attorney you may discover other specific rights and protections that are important to you.

## Making Decisions as Partners

The reality of the vast majority of partnerships I have seen is that legal voting provisions in the operating agreement have very little to do with actual decisions made by the partners. In fact, I have never observed a formal partner vote in an advisory firm. This is not to suggest that you should not carefully structure your voting process and specific rights (see above), but in reality you want to discuss how you will make decisions as partner on a day-to-day basis. Realistically, outvoting your partners consistently will create a toxic environment in the firm very quickly. At the same time, seeking consensus on every issue is impractical and often paralyzing for real-world partnerships. Below are few suggestions that I have found practical:

- Hold partner meetings regularly and with great deal of discipline—It is difficult to be partners without constant and extensive communication. If you prefer to do things on your own and not coordinate with others, a partnership is probably not for you. At the same time, just being in the same room is not enough. It is great if from the very beginning the partnership can get in the habit of creating agendas for the meetings, sticking to the points of the agenda and not getting distracted, and seeking to make decisions rather than just "discuss." When deadlocks are reached, there should be someone who constantly asks the question "What should we do?" rather than "Why not do this?" or "Why do this?" Often in the busy schedule of operating a firm there is a tendency to skip internal meetings, including partner meetings. That, however, is very detrimental to the business. It is like skipping family dinners—pretty soon you find that the kids prefer TV to your company (not a good thing—just in case you are tempted).

- Give each other freedom to operate and make decisions—Having to ask for permission from your partners for every little decision can grow old really fast. After all, most business owners are very independent minded and do not easily submit themselves to the control of others. Constant committee decision making can wear down even the best of partnerships. There is also a certain tendency for each partner to play the "devil's advocate"—if I propose an idea, my partner instinctively feels that it is his role to look for holes in the idea. It is a natural reaction, but it may really kill your sense of enthusiasm.

- The best process for decision making is to agree on a certain scope of independent activities that you do not have to check with your partners about. For example, if you are the partner in charge of marketing, there should be some freedom to hire graphic designers, engage with consultants, redesign brochures, and so on that you can do without having to go through every detail with a committee. This will allow for faster and more effective decisions and less friction between the partners.

- Agree on a process for letting each other know when you have hit a deal-breaker issue—It is also important to notify each other when you have hit a deal-breaker—that is, an issue that is very important to one of the partners. The deal-breakers are not always apparent in a dialogue, and your partners may not know that you feel so strongly about an issue. Very often, the worst friction in a partnership comes from one partner not realizing how important an issue is for the other.

For example, I had a client where one partner had a strong opinion about preferring anonymous performance evaluations (real example) and never wanted to have a process that required him to personally sign comments on performance. He once had a very bad experience in a past partnership where he was always the "bad guy," and his partners would sugar-coat their comments to the point where he was coming across as irrationally critical. This was a different firm and his partners had no idea why he was so sensitive about this issue. They could not understand his point of view and kept pushing back, not realizing that this brought him such emotional pain in repeating this experience.

Good decision-making in a partnership is a combination of open dialogue, knowledge of the other partners and trust in their integrity, and a sound process. The process quickly becomes a habit if the new firm can be disciplined to stick to it. However, just relying on "natural" chemistry can lead to declining frequency of communications and potentially poor relationships between the partners. The same can be true about discussion regarding succession-discipline and dialogue are key.

## Buy-Sell Agreements, Retirements, and Breaking Up

A buy-sell agreement is an agreement for one partner to buy out the interest in the case of certain events occurring—usually death or disability. It serves as an insurance policy for the owners and is frequently funded by life insurance that is "cross-purchased"—that is, one partner is the beneficiary of the other's policy. Such agreements are a must—they provide protection for the equity you have created and prevent a very difficult situation if something were to happen. Usually, the agreement provides some guidance on how the equity will be valued. This can be in the form of a formula or simply specifying that a valuation expert will be used if the agreement becomes effective. In either case, it will be a good idea to share the agreement with your CPAs as well as a valuation expert to make sure that the method of payment is tax efficient and that the valuation is reasonable.

The valuation in a buy-sell agreement will be lower than the valuation for almost any other purpose. Imagine the circumstances—one partner is gone suddenly, clients and staff are shocked, the other partner is overwhelmed and lacks capacity to service all the clients. This is hardly the kind of scenario you will assign a high value to. This is why I would argue that the buy-sell valuation is not a good way to deal with orderly transitions such as retirement or slowing down.

I really don't believe that passive ownership can work in an advisory firm over the long term, and that once an advisor leaves the partnership, he or she should stop being an owner in the firm. Usually, the operating agreement will specify what happens if a partner leaves. Very often, the act of leaving is "penalized"—that is, the valuation on the buyout is lower than other scenarios. This serves to discourage a partner from retiring by merely exiting the firm and dumping all the work and clients on his or her partners. Needless to say, the buyout will generate a significant strain on the cash flow of the firm too, so you may want to specify that the firm has several years to make the payments.

## Communicating the Deal to Clients and Employees

Communicating the merger to clients and employees is a critical step for the success of the endeavor and should be carefully planned and executed. First of all, it is important not to disclose any of the plans before the deal is actually done. Speaking to clients and employees about a possible merger and then telling them that the deal did not happen will leave you with a black eye and undermine your credibility as an owner and decision-maker. Premature announcements can also create anxiety, especially among employees, at a time when you may not yet have the answers to alleviate the anxiety.

That said, there are certain key employees that may need to be involved in the planning stages of a merger and whose ideas and knowledge may contribute to the process. You also would not want your employees to find out that you are merging with another firm from a third party—this will communicate the wrong message about their involvement in the business and will ruin the atmosphere in the office. In other words, choosing the right moment to talk to employees is quite tricky. Nonetheless, I would offer the following rules of thumb:

• Leaders—Employees whom you consider leaders in the firm and whom you may consider as future partners can and should be involved with the merger discussion once you have established that you are in agreement with the other side over strategy and personal goals (steps 1 and 2 in the beginning of the chapter) and you see no significant reasons for concern in the data provided by the other side. They should understand that a deal is pending but not guaranteed. The involvement of the leaders will be tremendously helpful in the business planning stage. Ideally you are working with people who can put their own self-interest aside and focus on the bigger picture. If you see signs that your leaders can think of nothing else but how this will affect their career, that's a good sign that they are not really leaders in your business (yet). Needless to say, at some point you do need to explain to all employees what their new role and career path would be.

• Other employees—I would recommend that you don't disclose the merger to the rank-and-file employees until you have a signed deal and you have a clear plan for what the changes will be. While you want to enlist the support of every employee for the new venture, you should be prepared to give them a good level of detail regarding their position and other job details. Generally, the announcement should be matter of fact (done deal, nonnegotiable) while not being a cold shoulder. I admit that finding the balance between the two is very difficult. The best advice I can give is to think of telling your kids that you are going to Grandma's place in Montana for Thanksgiving—there'll be a lot of complaining, but you know at the end of it all they will have a great time.

I take it for granted that you will need to communicate the merger to your employees first before any announcements are made to clients. Doing the opposite will undermine your staff in the eyes of the clients and will also create an environment of severe distrust. You may think of some clients as close friends (and some may be), but please resist the temptation to discuss the deal with them! Once again, they will have questions you cannot answer as well as natural anxiety that you won't be able to alleviate.

Any announcement in person is much better than any letter or e-mail, no matter how well crafted they are. The best announcement of the merger you can do is in person. The more of your top clients you can personally meet with and discuss the merger with, the easier the transition will be. When a meeting in person is not practical, phone calls can do very well too. Letters and e-mails should be reserved only for clients you cannot reach because of time constraints or with whom you are willing to take a risk and damage the relationships. In fact, there might be clients you don't want to transition to the new firm.

Typically clients react well to a merger announcement but have a concern over the changes in the business. You may find that clients really enjoyed having this "best kept secret" service where they felt that their relationship with your firm was exclusive and special. The merger may feel threatening from that perspective. They may be happy for you and your business success but worried that you and your staff will become too "corporate" now and won't have time for them or that the other clients and advisors will change the atmosphere and culture of your firm. To address that concern, it is best not to change too many things at the same time even if some may look relatively insignificant—for example, the conference room, the logos, your business card, the people present in a meeting, and so on. These may seem like silly little things, but changing them may have a symbolic meaning for clients.

The best step you can take in the initial announcements is to present your new partners and staff to your clients and emphasize how they belong in your firm. Give them the "microphone" and ask them to speak about the culture of your firm and why they can relate to that culture. When I first joined, Fusion, as a co-owner and president, what really helped me in my relationship with our clients was the shared experiences I already had with them. Emphasizing that I had known my partner for a long time, the fact that I had actually worked with some of his clients before, and the fact that I had attended some of their meetings in the past went much further than any degree or other credentials I had.

Once you have had a chance to make the personal announcements and talk to clients, you can issue the more formal press releases and send the letters to vendors, referral sources, and anybody else. You should prepare a formal press release and communicate it to your broad network. It is also helpful to write several subsequent letters updating clients on what is happening (avoid dramatic language) and continuously to reintroduce and promote your new staff and partners.

As much as you will be busy with the merger for the next year, you want the process to be over for clients and employees as quickly as possible. One of the biggest mistakes people make is to keep talking about the transition and using it as an excuse or as a conversation point. Rather, start only using the new name, start referring only to the new firm, and avoid mentioning the "old times"—you don't want clients or employees to think of them as the "good old times." Essentially, you want to send the message that "This is done, we are already living in a new firm, and it is very exciting." Make the ghost of the old firm disappear as quickly as you can. Emotionally, that may be difficult to do, but it is essential for the success of the new firm.

Lastly, never ever, ever, ever express doubts or criticism of the merger in front of clients or employees, even if you are struggling with something. If you don't believe in the merger, they never will. If you are not sure about your new partner(s), talk to him or her—not to clients or employees. Complaining in public will destroy your relationships with your partner(s) AND with your clients and employees. You have a new firm and a new vision—focus the same enthusiasm and energy you poured into your own practice on this new venture.

## Notes

1. My degrees are in economics and finance, not in psychology, and no one will describe me as a thoughtful, warm, and embracing individual.
2. Please don't start with "strong management team" no matter how highly you think of your management skills.
3. In a technical sense only for 20 days, but Mark treated me like a partner for a long time so I will indulge in extending the period.

# CHAPTER 5

# From Silo to Ensemble

I must confess that I have been dreading and avoiding this chapter since I started writing this book. Changing a "silo practice"—a practice where each partner has their own book of business to a true team-based practice is very difficult. Hiring and grooming professionals to create an ensemble is a difficult and lengthy process. Merging practices to create a large ensemble firm is risky and requires careful analysis and due diligence. Yet, both appear so much easier than bringing together two silo practices that are already under the same roof. Eliminating the silo mentality requires somehow forgetting years, sometimes decades of history, habits, and various arrangements that have become ingrained in the way the firm works and how professionals see their practice. It takes seeing your colleague and co-owners in a completely new light, and for well-established, mature practices, this may be the hardest thing to accomplish.

My house in Seattle was originally built in 1906, and for most of its century-long history it was a rental duplex and even triplex. The neighborhood I live in is just blocks away from the University of Washington, so the small rental units were in high demand. I can tell you from experience that converting a rental triplex into a single-family home is one hard process. Everywhere you look there are signs of the history of separate units. For a while we even used to get three electric bills. We had two garbage cans. As we were re-siding the outside we found two boarded-up doors and one window. There were many times when dealing with the old house drove me to think it would be easier to just blow it up and start with new construction. It might be cheaper too!

Silo firms are like old houses. They have a long memory of separate employees and separate clients and separate ways of marketing. They have a complicated web of arrangements for who pays for what and when and how various expenses are split. Sometimes it is next to impossible to figure these arrangements out, but any attempt to change them is viewed by the owners with the utmost suspicion.

Of all the clients I have worked with who wanted to convert their silo firm to a true ensemble, I must confess that more than half failed to make the necessary changes and returned to their silo ways—perhaps with some minor changes. When the changes worked, they took many years of gradual but consistent improvement. In fact, just weeks ago (February 2012) a former client with whom I had worked in 2006 met me at a conference and told me that he could now say that the last remains of the silo firm were gone. Success for them took six years of hard, at times painful change.

This is not meant to scare you from changing your firm but rather to invite your patience with the process. Years of silo practice cannot be undone with a few days of change—it will take years to implement. If you are not reading this book cover to cover but rather using it as a reference, I would encourage you to also read the chapters on mergers and creating an ensemble culture (Chapter 4 and Chapter 7, respectively). The process of converting a silo to an ensemble is very much a cultural change. Unlike mergers, though, it does not have the benefit of the forced change and almost ritual "burning of the boards" that mergers present. Here the key is to be patient and determined to change—one employee, one bill, and one client at a time.

## Creating a Shared Bottom Line

All silo practices have some shared expenses and a way of dealing with those shared expenses. Typically there is a pool of such shared bills inclusive of rent, some of the employees, some of the office expenses, infrastructure, and other expenses. To pay for those, owners either sign-over some amount of money to a shared account, or in cases where one advisor is the "primary," the other will override some of their broker-dealer compensation or through some other mechanism pay for shared expenses. The bills usually get reconciled once a year and adjusted, and the amounts are renegotiated almost constantly.

This arrangement is not free of friction, but in the spirit of friendship and long-standing relationships advisors tend to figure it out. The resulting system of payments is often impossibly complicated, but as long as no one feels they are being taken advantage of, the logic of the relationship supersedes any accounting logic.

As much as this "expense sharing" arrangement can be criticized, you can use this pool of shared expenses as your first step toward creating an ensemble. The process is rather simple and boils down to this—overfund your shared account. If you were to put too much money in this shared pool of expenses, at the end of the year you will have some shared profit. The presence of the shared profit will almost force you to consider the critical ensemble issues:

- What are our roles and responsibilities in a shared practice?
- What do we do for each other that we can't accomplish on our own?
- How can we fairly compensate each other for what we do?
- Are there shared resources that we can both benefit from?

Before diving into the specifics of how the shared pool of money can work, we will need a short management accounting lesson. In a silo firm where two or more firms coexist under the same roof but as their own distinct profit centers, (firms within a firm) we need to find a way to allocate shared expenses. The expenses of such a firm can be divided into two categories—direct expenses and shared overhead. Direct expenses are those that are clearly attributable to one of the practices. For example, if I take my clients to lunch, this is a direct expense—these are my clients. On the other hand, if my partner and I take our shared receptionist to lunch, this is a shared overhead. If an employee works only for me, he or she is a direct expense. If an employee's time is split between me and my partner, he or she is a shared expense.

Obviously, we need to arrive at a fair method of allocating shared expenses to the two practices. Such cost allocation is the subject of much accounting study, but in advisory firms it tends to be a fairly simple process. Cost is driven by activity, and activity has a "driver," a factor that causes it to be higher or lower. For example, clients tend to create activity and therefore tend to be a good cost driver—the more clients you have, the more activity you generate. The more activity you generate, the more cost you have. Other such drivers are revenues, assets, employees, and accounts. Sometimes different activities are driven by different drivers. For example, real estate cost tends to be a function of the number of employees you have since they occupy work space. The same is true for IT support costs and HR costs. On the other hand, the use of support staff tends to be driven by the number of clients you have or even, perhaps more precisely, the number of accounts you have.

In most silo firms the expense drivers are as follows:

- Split expenses evenly—This is a good way of accounting for the expenses and is hard to argue with. It essentially says, "If you are in business you have to pay your share." This arrangement can create issues if the two practices are not of the same size or have drastically different activity patterns, for example, a high-net-worth practice combined with a mass-market firm.

- Pay proportionate to revenue—Another good way of splitting expenses, essentially equating revenue with activity and activity with cost. With similar practices this will work very well but requires periodic adjustments. If revenue can fluctuate quite a bit, the partners may find that they need a minimum contribution limit. What happens if one practice suddenly declines a lot in revenue—does the other pay all expenses now?
- Divide the staff expense as a direct expense and split everything else evenly—Since the staff represents the largest expense, this tends to improve on the typical 50−50 split if one practice tends to have a more support-heavy pattern of expenses.

If the practices identify and pay direct expenses first, including dedicated staff, then the shared overhead will tend to be in the 20 percent to 25 percent range as a percent of expenses. If staff are not allocated as direct expense and shared in the overhead pool, then the total overhead should be around 35 percent to 40 percent of the expenses.

The simplest way of making a step in the direction of creating an ensemble is to overfund the shared expense pool. For example, instead of funding the expense pool with 25 percent of your revenue, fund it with 35 percent of the revenue. If historically shared expenses have been at 20 percent of the combined revenue, fund the account with 30 percent of both practices' revenue. The result should be your first shared bottom line.

This may seem like a very artificial way to create a common profit, but sometimes the very experience of having a shared resource and shared interest may force you to act more like partners. Once you have this shared profit, you can actually begin to conceptualize how you will divide it. You have both given something up, so now how will you get it back? Questions to consider are the following:

- What are partner activities that benefit both practices and perhaps deserve compensation?
- Are there management responsibilities that should be encouraged?
- Have you made referrals to each other and should those perhaps be compensated?
- Rather than spending the money, is there a shared investment you can make? Perhaps a shared employee or maybe a marketing campaign?

Spending two or three years with a shared bottom line will give you a lot of experience and a framework for making the more drastic changes described next. If sharing 10 percent of the revenue is too scary and too much—start slower and go for 5 percent over the normal level of expenses. If you feel you are ready for bigger changes, start with 15 percent rather than 10 percent. The bigger the shared profit pool, the closer you are to an ensemble.

## The "Mine, Yours, and Ours" Model

As another transition step toward being an ensemble, many firms also create a shared pool of clients. Those relationships are recognized as being jointly owned and jointly serviced. Usually, the advisors maintain all of their "personal" clients, most of the clients they had before entering into the partnership, and then agree that past a certain date, all new clients will be considered new clients. This structure resembles much the expense-sharing arrangement we described above but with the added benefit of having specific clients associated with the shared expenses, not just an agreement to override revenue to the shared pool.

As the pool of shared clients grows, so does the importance of partnering and working together. Initially, the economics of the "mine" and "yours" client base will drive the vast majority of the advisors' income. However, as the shared client base increases, the final outcome may be determined more by the common clients. When that happens and assuming the arrangement is working well, the partners may simply choose to just convert all clients to "shared" status.

Such an arrangement should be fairly easy to set up and operate and is a good way of easing into an ensemble agreement. Unfortunately, it also has a couple of significant drawbacks—it may take a long time to become effective and it may always create a bias to "my clients." My grandfather lived through the forced conversion of Bulgaria into a Communist country in 1945. He lived in a small town high in the mountains. Most households at the time had a cow or even several. Once the Communist regime took over, the cows were nationalized. One of the farmers who used to look after his own herd was hired to now care for the "cooperative" herd. Grandpa told me, "All of the cows were supposed to be 'our cows'—not mine, not yours. Yet somehow George [the farmer] always made sure he first fed the cows that used to be his." The memory of ownership is extremely powerful. It is thus difficult for the advisors to forget which clients were "their own."

## Assign Management Responsibilities

One of the hardest issues silo firms experience is the reluctance of the partners to participate in management of the firm. Managing the firm takes a lot of time, and in a silo environment when the income comes from servicing clients and adding new assets, there is little incentive to manage. Still, if you are to have a firm together, someone has to manage it. As my wife reminds me—if we want to have a home together, someone has to clean it and fix it.

Some firms prefer to delegate management to one "administrative partner." This partner assumes the full scope of management responsibilities and lets the other partners focus on growing the business. It is understood that the administrative partner will have less of a chance to develop business and service clients, and there is usually some accommodation and compensation for this work.

A good way of compensating the managing partner is by creating a salary that pays for the management role. Typically the salary is in the $30,000 to $50,000 range with the obvious assumption that the management is not going to be a full-time job. Other firms sometimes agree to "put business in the name" of the management partner in the form of percentage overrides.

Having a dedicated manager has the benefit of specialization and sometimes utilizes the skills of a partner who has the interest and the experience to do the job well. On the other hand, it tends to create a sense of isolation where one partner feels as if he or she is the only person in the firm who cares about management. To avoid this, even if you have an "administrative partner" you should make sure that all partners are engaged in the management of the business.

## Share Client Meetings

No one will be more enthusiastic about your partnership with another advisor than your clients. Most clients are very pleased to have another set of eyes in the relationship and welcome the involvement of another professional. Sharing client meetings with your partner is a great way to introduce him or her to your clients and to clarify the role he or she will play in the shared practice. Usually this starts with shared meetings where both of you are present.

Some firms actually take the extra step and make sure that they rotate their meeting responsibility. For example, if the firm routinely does four meetings with each client per year, they will switch clients for one of the four meetings. This allows each advisor to develop a relationship with the clients and also exposes the clients to different sets of expertise and experience. Naturally, sometimes there is a resistance to this change. Some clients would rather not be serviced and introduced to another advisor. Firms should not overreact to such resistance, though. Giving up entirely on the idea only because a couple of clients are reluctant is not necessary.

## The Prenup

When taking the risk of breaking down the silo walls, advisors frequently want to know that if things fail they can put them back up. This "prenuptial agreement" gives them the confidence that in a worst-case scenario they can restore the prepartnership state. The reality is that the more complex and complicated the prenup is, the more unlikely it is that the partnership will really succeed. There will be many frustrating moments in the experience of managing a firm together, and the easier it is to access the "eject" button, the more likely you are to use it. "Burning the boats" is definitely a good way to focus everyone on the same goal, but it is very difficult to do psychologically, so some prenup arrangements are understandable.

The first step is usually an agreement to restore ownership of the clients each advisor originally brought into the firm. Especially if the advisors had used the "mine, yours, ours" model, restoring the original status quo is only challenging with respect to the "ours." Even in those cases, there is usually one partner who is clearly closer to the client or has become the primary advisor to the client. In such cases, that advisor usually buys out the income of the other partner.

For example, let's say Stuart and I have been partners. I brought 50 clients with $300,000 in revenue, and he brought 100 clients with $500,000 in revenue. We each kept our client base, and then we developed 30 clients together with $300,000 in revenue ($10,000 each). Upon splitting, we find that 20 of the clients prefer to work with Stuart (nobody likes me!) and 10 prefer working with me. I have a 50 percent share in the 20 clients Stuart is taking, and he has a 50 percent share in my 10 shared clients. My 10 cancel out 10 of his, so we only need to settle on the 10 extra clients he is taking. My share of those is 50 percent × 10 × $10,000 = $50,000 in yearly revenue. Usually, the settlement is for me to receive two more years of payments for my share after the split. This is not a very rewarding settlement for me, but I can't complain either.

Separating employees is also rarely a problem since in the short history of working together there is usually not enough time for employee relationships to really merge. I am assuming that the ensemble experiment did not last for a long time, but my experience has been that if you can last past the first three years, you will continue down the path of ensemble partnership rather than a split.

A more difficult issue is the lease on the office—especially if you no longer want to be in the same office together. This is where the sparks fly. Very often, one partner is on the lease and the other is not—don't make that mistake. Sign the lease together. This will make sure you do not get stranded for the lease if your partner leaves. Usually the partner who is moving out will pay his or her share of the lease for some period after or until the other party has had a chance to sublease it.

## Change Your Thinking

At the end of the day, all of the steps suggested above are simply that—steps. None of them individually or all of them collectively will make your firm into an ensemble. They will take you closer to your goal, but the final and most important transformation will come from your ability to change the way you think. Becoming a true ensemble means the following:

- Not thinking of clients are personal relationships and "assets" and starting to see them as a shared responsibility.
- Inherently trusting your partner to do the right thing and letting go of the need to control your partner.
- Being comfortable with not tracing the economic effect of every activity back to its origin.
- Seeing management and safety (compliance) as a vital function for the firm and valuing that function.

The change in thinking is more difficult than you think. I have been in many meetings where silo advisors have great discussions about their future as a firm and all the great things they can achieve together. Then somebody will say something like "Wait! What happens if I refer a client to Bob and then that client refers another client—shouldn't I get paid for that referral?" At that moment, the entire "kumbaya" spirit of the meeting flies out the window and the discussion is back to square one.

My former partner, Mark Tibergien, was telling me another client story. In the middle of one such "ensemble formation" meeting, Mark asked one of the partners, "If something were to happen to you, would you like your partners to manage your wife's money?" The advisor responded quickly, perhaps too quickly: "Absolutely not!" Needless to say, the meeting never recovered from there.

These anecdotes serve to point out how difficult it can be to change the way you think and how deep the silo mentality can be rooted in the way you operate. Changing your thought pattern is not an entirely conscious process in the sense that you may not always realize that you are behaving in a "silo" manner. The advisor in Mark's story did not make a conscious decision to offend his partners and tell them that he does not really trust them—it was more of an impulsive reaction. I guess therapists spend hours and hours changing their patients' thought patterns. I am no therapist and have no theoretical knowledge of that process, but it seems there are some obvious parallels. That said, my experience has been that if you want to change the way you think of your firm you need to:

- Change your language and insist on the right vocabulary. Make a concentrated effort to say "our," not "my." If you say "my" you will think "my." If you say "our" you will think "my" for a while but eventually your brain may yield.
- Repeat the ensemble story as a "mantra." Not literally. Don't walk around the office chanting. Still, if you keep repeating out loud why you are coming together and how it will happen, you will tend to believe it more and more. Such positive thinking techniques are common in sports (and sales). You will eventually believe what you say and if you believe it, you are more likely to make it happen.
- Set up regular partner meetings with the agenda of reviewing the "state of the ensemble." Don't reschedule and cancel these meetings but rather prioritize them. Be upfront about what works and what doesn't.
- Don't tolerate exhibits of silo mentality, including your own. There is always a tendency to excuse things that happen in the "heat of battle." Unfortunately, pretty soon the exceptions overwhelm the rule. Consistency in behavior is critical, and it should be made clear to everyone that further displays of the silo approach will be considered a problem.

Changing years and years of habits and attitudes is very difficult but not impossible. Many of the top firms in the industry started with a silo structure and were able to transform themselves into a well-integrated, cohesive firm. The process requires conviction in the goal, patience, and persistence. My son reminds me that Batman and Robin had a hard time coming together at first, and Wolverine continued to exhibit streaks for "silo" behavior pretty much through the last episode. Still, even superheroes can work together, so imagine you are the Justice League[1] and give it a try.

## Note

1. You can try "The League of Extraordinary Planners" if you prefer or the "Fantastic Four CFPs," or the "CFP-men"—something like that.

# CHAPTER 6

# Partner Responsibilities and Partner Compensation

They say that you "shouldn't fillet the fish before you catch it" and perhaps ensembles should not jump to discussions about partner compensation before issues such as strategy and compensation are tackled. The reason why I want to tackle this issue early in the book, though, is that no one seems to want to even come into the boat until they know which piece of the tuna they are getting.

Well-thought-out and well-structured compensation for the partners will go a long way toward ensuring the success of an ensemble firm. While much of my consulting practice consists of putting practices together, an almost equal amount of time is spent on breaking failed partnership agreements. A poorly structured compensation and equity plan is often one of the major causes for the failure.

## Labor versus Equity

Before we begin to discuss partner compensation, we will need to define "compensation" by establishing the difference between labor and equity. Let me explain! An owner in an advisory business receives two types of income:

1. Compensation for the job performed. This job can be lead advisor or chief investment officer or portfolio manager or a combination of several jobs. Arguably, we could hire somebody from the outside and pay him or

her some amount of money in the form of salary and bonuses to do the job of the owner. In other words, there should be some fair market value for the services that each owner performs. That value may be very high if the owner/advisor is the CEO and lead business developer, but still we should be able to find what the market pays CEOs who are employed by organizations they do not own and control and argue that this number represents fair market compensation for the services performed by the owner as an employee.

2. Return on the equity investment in the business. In addition to being an employee in the business, owners should receive a return on the equity they have invested. This "dividend" is independent of the job description or performance of the owner and is typically related to the percentage of the business the person owns.

Let's go through some examples that give us a chance to examine this concept. I once had a client firm where James and Patrick were 50/50 partners, but James generated most of the new business and had clients that generated more revenue than Pat's. Pat, however, was the founder of the firm and had been James's mentor for many years. The firm generated $1.2 million in revenue and had expenses of $400,000, so the two partners split $800,000 equally between them.

James at times felt that he was not being rewarded for his higher level of productivity. In fact, when he was not in the best of moods he would call me and tell me that Pat went golfing two days a week and that he was rarely in the office after 3:00 p.m. He also said that Pat had not brought in a new client since the last leap year. He was not sure why Pat was making as much money as he was, especially since James was routinely in the office on Saturdays and even Sundays and had not golfed in five years (he hated golfing, but that's not the point). Pat, on the other hand, will tell me that James was losing respect for the fact that Pat had created this firm and had gone without pay for years to bring the firm to where it was. He will also point out that he introduced James to every single source of referral he had.

You can see both sides to this story, but what should they do? Clearly they were starting to develop problems with each other those could escalate to threaten the relationship. Unless this compensation issue was resolved, the partnership might all come to a bitter end—a shame, given their history together. My suggestion was to start with trying to separate the income they generated from the equity they had in the business. Given the contributions they had both made to the business, it might not be a bad idea to assign a higher level of salary to James, or even a percentage of the business he generated (or both), but perhaps give Pat a higher level of ownership. I was equally surprised that they were paid the same for what they did as I was for their 50/50 equity ownership.

One suggestion was for James to have a higher salary—for example, $300,000 plus a percentage of the new business compared to $200,000 for Pat in return for lowering his percentage ownership—say, from 50 percent to 40 percent? That way as Pat is slowing down, he will still earn his return on equity for the years he has spent building the business, while James will have the earnings potential created by his business development efforts. It seemed a reasonable way to approach the issue to me and by no means the only possible compromise. Unfortunately they preferred instead to split their businesses in half and each went their separate ways.

Another client I was working with, Max, Doug, and Alicia, were partners in business. Max was the CEO and chief business developer, Alicia was the chief investment officer and managed all the portfolios, and Doug handled all the financial planning and managed most relationships with clients. They had $2.5 million in revenue and about $1.0 million in expenses before any compensation to the partners. Max had a salary of $500,000, Alicia had a salary of $450,000, and Doug had a salary of $300,000 Those salaries corresponded to the income they used to have when they were all brokers with the firm they all used to work for before they broke away and started their own firm. Beyond the salaries, they are all equal partners and therefore share equally in the profits of the firm.

Note what is happening with the interaction between compensation and equity. Even though they are technically equal partners, the income they derive from the business is anything but equal—the income available to partners is $1.5 million ($2.5 million in revenue less $1.0 million in expenses). Of that income, $1.25 million is distributed as salaries, so the "profit" the partners share is only $250,000. As a result, Doug's income is almost half of Max's, even though they are nominally the same percentage owners. What is wrong here?

While here we have a clear separation of salaries and ownership, we may have the wrong salaries. Salaries for executives in the advisory industry are not easy to establish, but chances are that $500,000 is excessive for a salary and perhaps so is the $450,000 Alicia is making. The logic for setting the salaries is also flawed—what they were making in a different firm with a very different set of responsibilities is hardly a reason for setting salaries in this firm. Perhaps the three should adjust their salaries to a market level—for example, in the range of $180,000 to $250,000 for Max and Alicia and in the range of $120,000 to $150,000 for Doug. This will create a much bigger pool of profits, which will reflect more accurately their intention to be equal partners. Or perhaps they did not mean to be equal partners and their initial contribution to the business was not equal? An argument could be made that perhaps Max and Alicia contributed more to the creation of the business (more clients, for example) and should therefore be larger percentage owners.

Last example, another client firm had 40 percent overhead and paid out 50 percent to 60 percent of the revenue (the higher the revenue, the higher the percentage) to the advisor who generated it—whether he or she is a partner or not. Adam, who owned the firm, had decided to retire and wanted to sell his equity to five of his best employee advisors (he had almost 20 working for him). He was shocked to find that they had no desire to buy the equity. Why do you think this was happening? Well . . . simply consider what they are buying. After paying overhead and the advisors, the firm kept at best 10 percent and in most cases barely broke even (100 percent revenue − 40 percent overhead − 60 percent payout = $0). What's the point of owning that business other than incurring the liability, the risk, and the hassle of managing it?

In all of these examples, note that compensation methods determine the profit available to owners, and the impact on profits is such that we cannot separate compensation and equity. If indeed income drives value, then compensation influences income to such a degree that it actually impacts the value of the firm. With that understanding in mind, we can approach the subject of setting partner compensation and ownership structure.

## Using Profit Centers or Silos

The first question to consider when setting partner compensation is whether your firm has identifiable "profit centers," such as businesses within the business that have their autonomous strategy, separate staff, and relatively separate clientele and therefore should have their own income statement (P&L). Do you believe these profit centers should continue and that they are in line with the strategy of the firm? Are they silos you are trying to eliminate or integral parts of the business? If you have such strategically important profit centers they will need to be incorporated in your compensation logic.

There are many reasons to structure profit centers within the business with the following being some of the more common examples:

- An investment management department that manages money for advisors and clients outside the clientele of the advisory firm.
- An institutional investment consulting division that works separately from the retail investment advisory clients.

- A retirement planning division and a wealth management division.
- An insurance division inside a wealth management firm.
- An advisory firm within an accounting firm.

There is a clear difference between the silos structure we have criticized and such profit centers. The silos are replicas of each other and replicate (unnecessarily) the same services to more or less the same clients. The profit centers represent different lines of business, different services, and often very different clientele. They could be stand-alone businesses, but there is a synergistic reason why putting them under the same roof enhances the strategy of the separate businesses.

Good reasons for creating profit centers include the need for a separate strategy, which while congruent with the strategy of the firm needs its own set of activities and resources; the need to measure the profitability of a service and make separate pricing and resources decisions; a distinctly different group of employees that have a separate career track and different organizational structure; and regulation that requires the separation of two businesses into separate entities (e.g., having an internal broker-dealer). While the reasons may be very good as to why the firm should have profit centers, profit centers never enhance integration within the firm and promote unity. On the contrary, they tend to encourage the separation of people, goals, and cultures and will create some sense of friction. The question is whether the benefits outweigh the cost.

Even silos may be a necessary evil, as much as we have criticized them for the separation they create, we also need to acknowledge that they often exist for a good reason. Some reasons include: the firm is in the process of combining two businesses and the silos are a transition step; there is a geographic separation between the businesses (e.g., one partner in Chicago and one in Phoenix), or simply each partner wants to reserve the ability to manage his or her own P&L and has no intention to fully integrate.

Needless to say, if profit centers or silos exist, it will be nearly impossible to ignore them for compensation purposes, and some significant portion of the compensation will be based on the results of the profit center a partner practices in. My experience has been that it is very important to leave a significant amount of profitability that each profit center contributes to the general partner pool in order to encourage collaboration. The same is true for silos; it is best to leave at least some portion of the profits going into the shared pool so that the firm avoids full fragmentation.

For example, imagine Stuart and Barry were partners. Stuart manages the insurance department and Barry manages the advisory department, and each department has its own P&L. Stuart and Barry each draw professional compensation of 40 percent of the business generated, and the overhead of each department is 40 percent of the revenue. In other words, each department generates a 20 percent profit margin (100 percent less 40 percent direct compensation and less 40 percent overhead). It will be great if Stuart and Barry agree that half of that profit will be contributed to the general pool and divided between them based on factors such as equity ownership, contribution to the overall business, management responsibilities, and so on. If all of the 20 percent is kept by the partner who manages that profit center, there will be no financial incentive to share with the other profit center and no sense of shared success (or lack thereof). Note again that if a partner keeps the profit of the profit center, the equity ownership of the overall firm becomes irrelevant since there is no firm-level profit interest at stake.

I won't go into too much detail about the methods for allocating shared overhead since there are whole books written on the topic of cost accounting. Typically, though, each silo or center will pay its own direct expenses (e.g., salaries to dedicated employees, cost of center-specific software, etc.), and then the expenses that are not directly associated with a profit center will be allocated based on a formula. The formula may allocate expenses by the number of employees in each profit center, the number of computers, the percentage of revenue generated and serviced, the square footage occupied, the number of clients, or a combination of these. Ideally, the allocation formula is straightforward and is agreed upon by all partners. If you don't understand the formula and you need your accounting firm to perform the calculation, you have gone too far.

## Setting Owner Base Compensation

"Base compensation" is the compensation an employee receives for doing his or her job. The definition is the same for owners—base compensation is the amount an owner receives for doing their job. The job, then, is the fundamental set of responsibilities that the owner has. This can be (and probably should be) documented in a job description. "Owner" is not a job description (although it often feels like one), and all owners are not going to have the same job descriptions. Most of the time, owners are going to have titles such as "lead advisor," "portfolio manager," "chief investment officer," and the like. Each of those can be found throughout the industry, and there are many professionals who are not owners who hold these positions. This will serve as the foundation for our estimate of owner base compensation—how much are nonowners in other firms paid for the same job?

## Salaries

Salaries are the most logical and straightforward method of compensating owners for their "job." After all, chances are this is how all the other staff are paid. We can also easily establish the salaries of nonowners in the same position. Any other compensation method will most likely encourage some level of "eat what you kill," which we argued many times is undesirable for ensemble firms. Perhaps the only exceptions are owners whose primary job is sales (business development) and who have very limited engagement in servicing clients. In such positions we are likely to find a lot more variable compensation (commission) and fewer salaried professionals.

There are several high-quality surveys of compensation in the financial advisory industry that can provide guidance on prevailing salaries to owners and nonowners. Such surveys include the Moss Adams Survey or Staffing and Compensation, which is compiled every other year, and the FA Insight survey of Staffing and Compensation, which is on the same schedule. Both surveys contain a plethora of information on prevailing salaries among independent firms.

According to the Moss Adams survey, lead advisors were paid salaries between $125,000 (median) and $192,000 (third quartile) in 2011. CEOs, for example, command salaries between $214,000 (median) and $285,000 (third quartile). Many other positions can be benchmarked using the survey information. As we will discuss in the bonus section below, some firms pay a base salary for all the owners and then have a system of "bonuses" for performing certain management responsibilities.

The survey information does not have to be THE salary assigned to the owners. What is average or median in the industry is not necessarily what is best for your firm. For example, the average American male is overweight by 17 lbs and watches 9 hours of TV a week. That probably is not what you should be doing. That said, the surveys can provide a good starting point for establishing the salaries in your firm. You can ask yourselves questions such as these:

- How do want to pay owners relative to the market—above average, top 25 percent, or some other way?
- How is our owner job description different from the job descriptions in the surveys?

- What are the factors that determine a specific salary within a range of salaries?
- How do we need to adjust the national averages to our specific geography?

Another important question is the percentage of total income you would want the salary to represent for the owners. Naturally, if the salary represents 90 percent of owner income, this will render factors such as equity ownership and bonuses less meaningful. On the other hand, if the salary represents less than 50 percent of the income, then this will significantly increase the importance of the bonus system and equity percentages. Finally, many partnerships also look at the base-level income needed by the partners to maintain their lifestyle and set the salary to meet that income. That's a bit arbitrary since the lifestyle cost is a very personal decision, but if there is an agreement about a number between the partners, this is not a bad method.

## Payout Systems

Rather than a salary, many firms use a percentage of revenue to pay their partners. Usually this is done in silo firms where each partner has his or her own client base and an identifiable stream of revenue that they generate. Obviously this is a system that promotes silos and therefore dampens the potential for integration, but it may be a system that is logical and natural in the beginning of an ensemble firm.

If a payout is going to be the prevailing compensation method, my suggestion would be once again to look at the compensation of nonowner lead advisors as a guideline for compensating the owners. Experienced advisors who work in wirehouses receive between 40 percent and 50 percent payout for being the lead advisor in the employment of the firm. This is probably a good starting point for independent firms. It also leaves enough profit potential to create a meaningful pool of shared profits. Typically the overhead expenses of a firm should be around 35 percent to 40 percent, leaving 10 percent to 25 percent in shared profitability (100 percent less 50 percent payout, less 40 percent overhead = 10 percent or 100 percent − 40 percent − 35 percent = 25 percent). Even though the payout encourages the silo separation, it may be creating enough shared economics to bring the partners together "at the bottom line." Needless to say, if the payout is set at a high point, for example, 70 percent, it will wipe out any potential for shared profits.

## Draw Systems

Since salaries and payouts are paid regularly but bonuses and profit distributions are made once or twice a year, some owners may struggle with the discrepancy between their total income and their regular income. This is especially true if the salary is a relatively smaller portion of the total income of the partners.

For this purpose, some firms allow partners to "draw" a percentage of their anticipated or historic income as a regular income stream, rather than wait for the bonus and/or distribution determinations. For example, let's say Jonathan has a salary of $200,000 and last year got a $160,000 distribution from profits. Then the firm may let him draw 80 percent of that total income on a monthly basis so that he has more regular personal cash flow. The draw amount will be 80 percent times $360,000 (last year's income) = $288,000. Jonathan can now get $24,000 a month in "draw" as opposed to his salary, which is $16,667 per month. At the end of the year, his income will be "trued up" with the new profit levels. So, for example, if he gets a $200,000 profit distribution this year, he will get a check for $112,000. This is the result of $400,000 in total income ($200,000 salary + $200,000 profit) less his draw of $288,000 already paid = $112,000 at the end of the year. His draw for the following year will then be 80 percent times $400,000 = $320,000.

Note that I have completely ignored taxes in this discussion. Ignoring taxes, however, has gotten many in trouble, and you should take a look at how you will pay taxes. Since partner income is not subject to withholding at the paycheck level (assuming you like most advisors have elected a pass-through entity), you should have a system for either paying personally estimated taxes as advised by your tax professional or, if you are paying them from the firm, you should incorporate the taxes into the draw calculations. Many practitioners get in trouble by not factoring taxes when they draw their income and then finding that the partnership does not have cash to make estimated tax payments.

## Benefits

Finally, owner benefits should be considered as part of the compensation package and should be consistent with the rest of the pay process. The benefits are usually the same for all owners, and it is usually a good idea to be consistent with the types of benefits available to employees. I generally dislike systems that overuse benefits. Some firms create very expensive benefit packages for their partners in an effort to maximize the tax effect. Such heavy benefit packages typically serve older partners better than younger ones who prefer more cash. They may also overspend in the sense of putting more dollars into benefits than partners would have spent if the money were coming directly out of their pocket. The same is true for perks. There is a clear tendency to overspend on perks because it is "company money" and not coming out of the partners' checkbook directly.

## Owner Bonuses

If base compensation rewards the fundamental responsibilities, owner bonuses reward specific results. Bonuses are not always necessary for owners—after all, the profits are the ultimate performance-based reward system. Still, if there are differences between the ownership of the business and the contribution of the partners, the bonuses are a good way to reconcile such discrepancies. For example, if an advisor is only a 10 percent owner but is contributing 40 percent of the revenue of the firm, a bonus for new business development may be a good way to reconcile his contribution to his income without putting strain on the equity arrangement. It should be noted, though, that the bonus may be a short-term fix in such a situation and that the firm may still need to change the equity ownership in the long term.

The most common bonus methods are the following:

- Management responsibility premium—Many firms pay a salary premium to the partners who handle the administrative responsibilities for the firm. Such responsibilities may include being the managing partner, the chief compliance officer, the chief operations officer, chief investment officer, and others. In such cases, the partner who takes on these responsibilities may receive an additional $50,000 in salary (CEOs, managing partners) to $30,000 (CCOs, COOs, CIOs). Such premiums are not set based on any specific analysis but rather the estimate of the partners of the demands of the job. The amounts above are pretty typical but do not represent a survey or my recommendation—just a common practice. Note that technically this is pay for the job responsibilities of a partner and thus it can be argued that it is not a bonus but rather part of base pay.
- Business development bonus—Business development continues to be the Achilles heel of many firms, and while advisory businesses no longer overvalue business development (the hunter-gatherer past we discussed in Chapter 1), they still need to incentivize those that generate new client relationships. It is not uncommon for firms to pay 5 percent to 15 percent

of the ongoing revenue to the partner who first created the relationship. Alternatively, partners may receive 20 percent to 30 percent of the revenue as a one-time bonus for a new client relationship. Again, these percentages are based on my experience and are not statistics or recommendations. Note that they are much lower than what the referral payment will be for an external source of referral.

- Profit center percentage—If there are profit centers in the firm, those are difficult to ignore, and usually there are bonuses to the partners running a profit center based on the results of that unit. Usually 30 percent to 50 percent of the unit profits are retained within the partners representing the unit. Systems that pay more than 50 percent of the profits of the center to the partners who operate it tend to lean heavily in the silo direction.
- Cross-referral incentives—There are often bonuses that encourage cross-referral between different services in a firm. For example, in a firm that has an accounting division and a wealth management division, it is very common to pay the partners generating the referral 5 percent to 15 percent of the first-year revenue (note that these are lower than the external sale bonuses). Such bonuses are particularly common in large firms with many partners where the participation in the general partner pool may be heavily diluted and therefore not an effective link between the referral and the compensation.

## The Role of Equity Ownership in Income

As we said in the beginning of the chapter, owner income should be a balance between contribution and equity. Systems that reward equity too much tend to emphasize tenure, percentage equity owned, capital contributed, and so on but tend to undercompensate new sales, intellectual capital, relationship management, and so forth. Systems that focus on contribution tend to underestimate the importance of bearing risk, managing the business for the long term, contributing capital, and being loyal. A good system will be somewhere in the middle as you can see in Figure 6.1.

I very much believe that once the equity structure of a firm has been set and has been in existence for some time, it becomes very difficult to change it. Changes to the ownership of a firm can be very disruptive and the process

**FIGURE 6.1**  Equity and Contribution Are the Two Opposing Forces of Owner Income

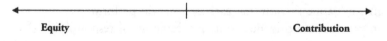

Equity                                                                 Contribution

is always very uncomfortable for the owners. That's why I would generally advise clients to look first at ways through which they can use the compensation system to address existing income issues and then follow a more gradual transition over time rather than making one-time disruptive changes. That's why it is very important to set the initial ownership with a long-term view in mind.

## Discretionary Expenses and Perks

They say that "good fences make good neighbors." My advice is—don't play with the fence. It is a common practice among advisors to run a variety of discretionary expenses through the business. This includes car payments and gas, restaurant bills, family cell phones, and so on. My advice to clients regarding such "perks" is pretty straightforward: "DON'T!" The discretionary expenses create potential friction within the partnership; they encourage spending, distort the financial record, and potentially create problems on your tax return. The benefit is usually minimal while the damage can be fairly substantial. Not to mention the potential troubles with the tax-code.

What is more, often advisors end up spending significantly more on items they run through the business compared to what they would spend if they had to reach in their own pocket and pay with their own credit card. The "company money" becomes like "play" money—it is easier psychologically to spend it. This may even create personal financial issues. For example, in 2009 when the market was in deep recession, advisors were trying to reduce cost throughout the business and cut expenses, only to find that the first expenses they needed to cut were their own personal ones—a double hit at a time when their income was severely reduced.

## Partner Compensation Discussion Worksheet

If you are discussing partnership compensation and equity structure as part of a merger or acquisition, or simply revisiting your own agreement, I would offer the following sequence of questions as a framework for that discussion. Simply ask these of yourself and your partners.

### Start with compensation first, rather than equity:
- Can you define the job that each of you will perform?
- Can you assign a title and create a specific set of responsibilities?

- Can you assign a salary to the job or is it better compensated on a variable basis (i.e., commission or a draw)?
- What is the prevailing salary in the industry for this position or these positions?
- Is it desirable to have a performance bonus for the owners based on their individual performance or the performance of their division? Which one or both? Can you measure performance and how?
- If a bonus is a good idea, how significant will the bonuses be as a percentage of total compensation to that person?
- Can you live with one of you getting a big bonus while the other is not receiving much of a bonus—for example, a great year for benefits and a bad year in personal financial advice?

### Do you need profit centers where each practice will retain some level of P&L?

- Why do you need profit centers?
- They will certainly hinder integration to some degree, but they can be very beneficial in measuring success, providing incentives, and keeping a clear view of the economics. In total, is the benefit higher than the cost?
- How will you allocate the shared cost that is common for profit centers? By headcount, by revenue, by computer, by square footage, or by some combination of these?
- What happens to the profits of each profit center? What percentage will go to the shared pool and what percentage will be retained?
- The profits from the profit center can be used to fund the owner bonus.
- Talk to your attorneys and accountants—is there a reason to use separate entities for the profit centers? Separate entities will damage integration badly but there may be a compelling marketing or legal reason?
- Do you anticipate in the future someone being an owner in one but not the other(s) profit centers?

### Equity ownership (save for last):

- What will be the guiding principle behind the combination? Will you use (1) profits contributed (need to clean up and define); (2) revenues contributed (are they equally profitable?); (3) valuation estimates to determine the percentage ownership?
- Will ownership be fully proportionate? Is there any disproportionate feature such as preferred profit interest, voting rights, or redemption rights?.

- What decisions will be subject to supermajority vote (effective veto)—please consider these carefully.
- How and when will you distribute the profit of the company? This becomes very important if you forgo salary and benefits as methods of compensation and simply draw on your share of the owner income.
- Who is responsible for past liabilities (financial and legal) of each respective entity? Will each party take care of their own?
- Does any of the businesses need a capital infusion for example, purchases of equipment, new systems, and so on? Who will contribute capital? Will capital contribution mirror ownership of the business or interest in the profit center (if applicable?)
- Discuss this agreement with your attorneys.

# PART II

# Managing an Ensemble

# CHAPTER 7

# Creating Ensemble Culture

My favorite definition of culture is that "culture is what happens when no one is watching." What people do in the absence of direct supervision and the punishment-reward system of management is truly revealing of the values they hold and who they are as professionals. This is why culture is that "invisible hand" that truly regulates the behavior of a firm and more or less determines whether the firm will succeed or fail in its strategy. I know Adam Smith proposed that economic decisions (demand and supply regulated through pricing) govern market behavior, but I would propose that culture is governed by what people truly believe is wrong and right and less by money. Creating the right culture will always make a firm successful. The question is—how can you manage something as elusive as human behavior, especially behavior that you can't see—that is, when you are not there.

I can make this a very short discussion—the most effective way to influence the culture of your firm is by setting an example. What you, as the owner(s), do (not what you say) will have a much larger impact on how your people behave than any other consulting exercise, corporate retreat, and posters on the wall. In fact, it will have an overwhelming influence on the firm, and the firm will reflect who you really are as a person and as a professional. Perhaps that is different from who you thought you were. If you read nothing else in this chapter, this is what you need to remember—your firm will behave exactly as you do. You know how they say that after a while a dog starts looking like its owner? Well . . . after a while a practice starts behaving like its owner too.

Having made this very strong statement, I need to also make an important note of disclosure. In management studies, at times it is very difficult to identify the source of the recommendation—is it a survey, is it the author's experience, is it a case study, and so on. Very often, the prescriptive tone of the message ("You must do this unless you are crazy") is a substitute for a source of the recommendation. This is particularly true for "soft" topics like corporate culture, which are very difficult to research with an academically rigorous methodology. From a source perspective, the recommendations of this chapter are entirely and fully based on the experience of the author—yours truly. There is no research or surveys behind it, other than my personal observations of a couple of hundred firms that I have worked with or in some cases worked for. In other words, I am not expert in this field—I am a patient of this hospital just like you are. Sometimes, though, patients can learn a lot by exchanging stories.

## Establishing Priorities and Values

Implicit in every decision is a set of values that the person making the decision believes in and follows. Take a simple example. One of your colleagues looks at her calendar and notices that a call with a client is scheduled for exactly the same time when she is also supposed to go to lunch with you—the CEO of the company. Clearly, she can't attend both, so she has to choose one. In choosing, she will reveal something about her values and priorities. What is more important, the client meeting or the meeting with the CEO? Who is likely to be more flexible—the CEO or the client? How do you build a career in your firm—by talking to the CEO more often or by talking to clients more often?

This may sound like propaganda, but the little choices we make all day and every day will have a much higher level of impact on organizational culture than any of the big statements we make in staff meetings. If you are the owner, your choices reveal to employees what is important to you, and employees will inevitably follow those priorities. For example, if you routinely check e-mails and voice mails while on your vacation, then employees will certainly perceive a similar expectation to always be in touch with the business. If the first question you ask about any project is always "How much will this cost?" you will find that employees are becoming similarly cost conscious. If you are always rescheduling internal meetings in favor of other engagements, they will do the same. If you routinely schedule personal errands during business times, employees will likely perceive that they can do the same.

I have heard many business owners say "They [employees] understand that I am an owner and they are employees" as a justification for why they can do some things employees cannot. Unfortunately, that's rationalizing, not justifying. This logic is very similar to telling your kids to not smoke and not drink while you are holding a glass of whiskey in one hand and a cigarette in the other. It never works and it never will.

This creates psychologically a very difficult conundrum for business owners. Many look at this difficult requirement to modify their own behavior and start feeling as if the business is starting to control them, rather than their controlling the business. "What's the point of owning a business if I can't do what I want to do? I might as well work for a bank!" Personally I feel that your own business gives you the chance to instill and convey the values that really matter to you but at the cost and concession of removing some of your habits and preferences that can harm the business. For the price of modifying your behavior a little, you can do what matters to you the most. If you can't do that, you have to accept that employees will do what you do and learn to live with the consequences. If you can't stop smoking, you have to be prepared that your kids will smoke too.

The shared values of the firm tend to be unclear at first but over time as the ensemble firm grows they become well established. After six to seven years of history, it is common to hear employees use phrases such as "That's not how we do things," or "We have always done it this way." From that point, values will continue to clarify and evolve, but it will be more and more difficult to change how the firm behaves. In other words, as you are growing your firm, it is very important that you pay attention to the culture in the office early because later it might be difficult to change.

Values are communicated to new employees through the actions and statements made by the owners and their peers. Most people, over time, adopt and conform to the culture in the office rather than change it. This has important implications about your staffing policy. If there is an employee or group of employees that do not behave according to your expectations, they are very likely to influence others. In fact, they are more likely to change newcomers than newcomers are likely to influence them. In other words, if there is an influence in the office that you are not comfortable with, don't tolerate it and eradicate it as soon as you can because it will only promulgate itself. Sports teams are particularly attuned to that influence. You hear coaches talking about a "culture of losing," and you often see them trading away a lot of players they inherited. They do that not because they are bad players but rather in an effort to remove the influence they will have on new players brought in to improve the team.

The key components of the culture, in my experience, tend to center around the following:

- How we perceive and deal with customers.
- How we relate to each other and how we treat each other.
- How we measure performance and effort and how we reward it.
- How we deal with conflict internally.
- What variance we tolerate from the norm.
- What the "centers of influence" are in organizational culture and how uniform they are.

Let's examine each factor in turn.

## Customers—Service as Culture

If you ask a group of financial advisors what distinguishes their practice, you are very likely to hear the same word from 99 out of 100 advisors—"service." All advisors pride themselves on the service they provide, and no advisor will ever say that service is not important. Indeed, service is a very powerful differentiator, and a firm with a strong service culture will have a tremendous advantage over any competition. However, the same is true for hotels— every hotel manager will tell you that he or she first and foremost focuses on service. Still, as you can probably ascertain from your personal experience as a consumer, hotels rarely distinguish themselves by their service. In fact, most could improve it significantly. Chances are the same is true for most advisory practices. Without hurting your pride, I would invite you to consider if client service is really at the core of your culture. See how these simple questions apply to your company.

Do you focus on what the client needs rather than on what your firm does, doesn't do, or how you do it? Clients rarely understand all the complexity of operations of our industry or the process that the industry follows. They tend to have requests that are expressed in their own vocabulary or terms and that are driven by their needs. If we substitute those needs with our own complex operational procedures, we risk completely alienating the client. The killer phrases of client service are "Our system does not allow," "My computer won't," "It's our policy not to. . . ." Instead, the staff should have the attitude that every client request is legitimate and that it is our job to understand that request and respond to that need within our processes and procedures.

Do you tend to pass the puck? If you would like to lose as many clients as you can, as quickly as you can, your best bet is to have your staff repeatedly forward the client to somebody else. There is no other phrase that can kill client relationships as quickly as "Let me put you through to . . . who can do that for you." Clients rarely understand fully the specialization in an office and they rarely would know exactly whom to call. Most clients would like to rely on their regular contact to walk them through the corridors of the firm to get things done. Ideally there is a mentality in the firm that "whoever has the ball is the quarterback"; that is, if you receive a client request you need to see it through to completion and not just forward the request.

Do your advisors have a sincere and genuine interest in and focus on the person in front of them?. There is no disappointment bigger than realizing that the person right in front of you is not focused on what you are saying but is thinking of something else or doing something else. If you have ever had an experience in a hotel or a store where you are standing in front of a service person (your credit card in your hand) and looking at him or her, while the person proceeds to talk on the phone or to a colleague, you know what I am talking about. Undivided attention is a rare gift today in the presence of so many screens and devices. Still, it may be the key to the best client meeting you have had. If your staff can ignore everything else for an hour while they are meeting with a client, then you will find that clients will reciprocate with loyalty and will help your practice to succeed. Being interrupted, distracted, or hurried is the sure recipe for achieving the opposite.

Do you have real knowledge of the client? Early in my career I worked with a remarkable CPA partner and professional -- Ed Drosdick. Ed told me one day, "It is not so important to remember the names of the client's kids or dogs, but I try to remember everything there is to know about their business, who their employees are, who their clients are and what keeps them awake at nights." Having such in-depth knowledge of the client's financial affairs is not just a function of a good CRM and a decent memory; it is the product of a deep interest in the client and enjoyment of one's work. When you demonstrate that level of knowledge, clients are not only impressed but also eager to share more.

Can you do the right thing when things go wrong? Things will eventually go wrong in every service business—a letter will get lost, a piece of information will be mis-recorded, a change will not get made. Sometimes the mistake is trivial and sometimes it can be serious in dollar terms. Businesses that have the ability to accept responsibility for their mistakes and quickly focus on fixing them tend to have much better client relationships and are much less likely to lose clients as a result of their mistakes. This may seem like a self-evident statement, but in most businesses the employees are quite reluctant to accept responsibility for a mistake and are often defensive when something goes wrong. Even if the issue gets escalated to the owners and resolved at that level, the initial defensive reaction is likely to get the client's blood boiling.

Can you act against your selfish interest? Doing something for a client because it helps you to be profitable is not going to earn a lot of loyalty from the client. Doing something for a client because it is best for them even if it hurts your self-interest is something they will always remember. Covering a cost you didn't have to cover, waiving a fee you didn't have to waive, reducing a cost you didn't have to reduce creates a tremendous sense of trust with that client. A client who sees you go against your profit motivation in order to help them will give you their loyalty and their business for many years to come.

Are you faking it? At the end of the day, client service focus is not something your firm can fake. You can put any kind of "mission statement" messages on the wall and make as many speeches in the staff meetings as you want—if the service is not at the core of the culture, clients will recognize that you are just going through the motions. The only way that service becomes part of the DNA of the company is through the owners' personal example. If the owners are doing everything they can to help clients and if they are sincere in their efforts, then employees will follow. If the owners are going through the protocol but in private often complain about clients being "needy," the staff will do exactly the same.

It should be noted that client service is almost by definition inefficient. All of the principles of service culture we are describing are potential inefficiencies. Call centers are a very efficient form of client service. They are also universally hated by all of their clients. Small family restaurants are always terribly inefficient in their output of food and their table turnover. They are also loved by their clients, who would go out of their way to praise them and will go back again and again in lean times and times of prosperity. Service culture is a powerful differentiator, but it is not a friend of efficiency.

## How We Deal with Each Other

One of the most important "silent statements" culture makes is how the employees of a company relate to one another and how they treat each other.

Solo firms tend to have a very family feeling, with all employees defining their group position through their relationship with the "patriarchic" figure of the advisor (or "matriarchic"). The advisor takes care of everybody and is involved in all relationships. There is usually some "sibling rivalry" type of friction in the firm, which the advisor will always break up but perhaps inadvertently encourage by making her or his attention one of the bigger prizes in the office. Well . . . you can't do that in an ensemble firm—you have to create a different model of interaction and relationship—families just don't work with such a large number of "parents."

While installing hierarchy in a small firm may seem awkward and unnecessary, some understanding of status in the firm becomes necessary. It is simply impractical for the owners to be involved in every interaction and serve as the decisive vote in every decision. What is more, the multiple owners may have different perspectives and different opinions, making it even more difficult for them to play that paternalistic role. In other words, employees will have to make decisions and operate based on a different protocol than the family meeting.

Demonstrations of hierarchy are usually corrosive to the culture of the firm, but it is very important that everyone in the firm understands who the senior people are and who is reporting to whom, as long as such relationships exist. Carefully maintaining and supporting this nascent hierarchy should be a priority, especially since the more junior staff are very likely to try to undermine it and create a direct relationship with the owners. If you allow for that to happen, you will destroy your own ability to operate without personal involvement and you will sabotage the firm's growth. Unless you want to be involved in every operational decision and task, don't step between the line managers and their staff and create a "bypass."

Hierarchy, of course, is only one aspect of the relationships between employees. Another factor that will heavily influence the culture of the firm is the degree to which teamwork and team collaboration is valued. In firms where teamwork is seen as one of the top characteristics of a successful employee, the environment tends to be much more collaborative and free of conflict. In firms where individual achievement and contribution is valued highly, there is always a tendency for competition and friction. If you extend this further, there are firms where individual achievement can completely trump teamwork in the evaluation of an employee and in those firms, conflict is a frequent visitor.

I have worked with and inside firms where the phrase "He is so smart that he has trouble working with others!" is almost considered to be praise. It is used to describe the brilliant CFAs and CFPs or the maverick business developers who seem to treat their colleagues as being at a lower level of intellectual or professional ability. As a result, they treat others with impatience and sometimes contempt. The other side reciprocates with sabotage and an equal level of contempt. Frequently, the result is a tacit understanding that "David does not play well with other kids."

What kind of behavior between employees is tolerated sends a very clear signal to all staff. If you tolerate David's sense of superiority and contempt for his co-workers, you are inviting conflict and trouble putting teams together. Usually, as an owner, all you need to do is to make it clear to David that you will simply not tolerate such behavior, no matter how smart you are. Bob DiMeo, the founder of DiMeo Shneider, a large RIA and institutional consulting firm, calls this the "no a-holes rule."

Ideally, the atmosphere in an ensemble firm is similar to the atmosphere of a successful sports team. There is clear recognized high authority that sets direction for the firm—the coaches—that is, the partners. There is a sense of camaraderie between the players and the intuitive understanding that we win together and lose together. This understanding that no one can win individually unless the team wins brings even the most individualistic people together. Finally, there is an established system of "captains"— formal or informal—that "coach" on the field, where the coaches cannot be physically present. Sometimes those captains are formally appointed by the coaches (hierarchy), but sometimes they just emerge and become universally accepted. For that dynamic to occur, though, the owners (the coaches) have to create the right atmosphere, set the right example, and of course, win some games. Nothing destroys the culture of a team as losing a lot of games. One or two losses can strengthen and improve a team; a long streak of losses just takes its life out.

## Performance as Part of the Culture

Every firm evaluates the performance of its employees. Whether that is through a formal performance evaluation system or a system of closed-door conversations between the partners, there is some process of performance evaluation and employees know it. Firms that perform the evaluation in an open and constructive dialogue tend to create an environment where feedback is expected, appreciated, and acted on. Firms that "whisper" their critical comments behind closed doors tend to create an environment where every critical comment is seen as a personal attack.

I am a big believer in creating an atmosphere of open but constructive criticism in a firm. One of the best tools for such feedback is a formal performance evaluation process. It is not the only mechanism, though—many of those conversations can be part of staff meetings and other project meetings. The key is to be clear regarding the nature of the criticism and constructive with suggestions for improvements. Public castigation is not the goal here and is counterproductive. Accountability and responsibility are the goal—not shame.

Criticism implies also setting a standard, and the standards for performance are very much part of the culture of a firm. There are many different possible statements about performance and they describe very different firms. For example, compare the following statements:

"He tries very hard and does everything he can."—Effort based, not comparative.

"No one works harder. She is always the last to leave the office."—Effort based, comparative, offers a specific measure.

"He has hit every goal we set for him."—Results based, goal was set by the firm and used as a criterion, not comparative.

"She has the highest revenue under management of all advisors."—Numeric, comparative, results based.

There are many firms where effort is the criterion ("He does all he can and he has really improved!"). This tends to create a somewhat complacent environment where a lot of the more ambitious projects are never completed and where high achievers tend to get frustrated. In such environment the job does not always get done but as long as everybody "tried" there is no criticism. Since this is how family members usually evaluate one another, this is a very natural tendency for most firms. Unfortunately, as the firm grows it has to eventually combine effort with results. "Friendship is no substitute for getting the job done!" says Bill Murray in an interview.

Whether you focus on effort or results, the worst mistake you can make is to judge different employees differently. What often happens in firms that grow quickly is that the staff gets split into "family" who are treated under the family criteria and "new people" who are treated under result-driven criteria. Loyalty is commendable, but such a culture is very dysfunctional and frustrating to all. When some employees feel that they are constantly under the gun while others are commended for subpar performance as long as they "put their heart into it," there is bound to be some animosity between the groups and ensuing turnover among both groups. You have to consider that the family usually don't want to be considered less capable and chronic underachievers.

## Conflict

Some level of friction and even conflict is practically unavoidable in a growing firm, and therefore ensembles are extremely likely to encounter a "period of turbulence." It seems to me that the best reaction in such instances is a measured response that emphasizes teamwork but lets conflict run its course. Many owners overreact, by literally separating the employees, and never letting them work together again. This creates a strange workflow in the firm that is designed to bypass the interaction between two people rather than maximize efficiency or client service.

Just because a couple of people go through friction does not mean that they cannot work with each other ever again. On the contrary, there are studies suggesting that some conflict early in the relationship allows people to learn how to deal with difficult situations together. Overreacting and stepping in the middle denies them that chance.

On the other hand, if a conflict is turning into a feud where both parties do not seem to be seeking any resolution other than engaging their time and emotion (and all others') in warfare, then it is usually time to step in and declare that enough is enough.

## Promotions

One of the most critical values in an organizational culture is the "promotion preference." Some firms tend to look very hard internally at candidates for promotion into an increased role, while others will immediately meet the need by hiring outside. The internal bias tends to create loyalty, career tracks, and a sense of upward mobility. The external track brings much needed expertise and an influx of external ideas. There is a tendency for small firms to become 100 percent "home-grown," which results in inefficiency, suboptimal ideas, and often missing vital components. Much like the Maya, who had a very sophisticated civilization but somehow had not invented the wheel yet, the home-grown firms can be missing significant systems or processes.

My experience has been that there needs to be some influx of external talent in a firm and some understanding that the career progress is not a ticket-window line. The statement that expertise and performance are critical for success in a firm is not always clear and apparent to employees. Especially in firms that value loyalty highly, there is a strong tendency to assume that if you got there first, you get promoted first.

## Who Owns the Client?

The owners of many firms approach client ownership as a legal issue, but in reality little can be done to stop advisors from leaving and taking clients with them unless the firm truly has a culture of institutional ownership of the relationships. If the firm has a culture that tolerates and even encourages statements such as "my clients," "my revenue," "my referral source," and so on, the legal barriers to someone leaving with clients are likely to prove rather weak. What is more, the threat of leaving with clients is sometimes a much bigger issue than the actual execution of that threat.

A culture of shared ownership of the clients, like many other cultural values, starts with the owners and the example they set. Advisors who grow and develop their career in a firm that promotes firm-level ownership are very unlikely to even consider taking clients away from the firm. It will just seem like an unnatural act to them. I spend the first 10 years of my career in Moss Adams LLP—the largest accounting firm on the West Coast and a firm with a wonderful culture of shared client ownership. The firm had the concept of stewardship—the partners are stewards of the client relationships on behalf of the firm. As stewards they have the emotional and ethical obligation to do everything they can to help the client. At the same time, the firm made it clear that clients are not "owned" by the partners, that relationships can change from one partner to another, and that the firm would not tolerate any challenges to the collective "property right."

Having "grown up" in that culture, it never occurred to me or any of my peers that partners might leave and take their clients with them. We certainly saw partners leave the firm, but they rarely even attempted to keep their clients and when they did, they usually bought their clients from the firm. Literally, partners who left to establish an independent practice will pay the firm for the right to bring their clients with them. Younger partners would take this stewardship model pretty much for granted and would not even think of challenging it.

The factors that tend to enhance that culture of stewardship rather than ownership are the following:

- Incorporating peer reviews in the client service process—Peer reviews of the work are a great way to enforce process integrity and manage risk.
- Encourage team service—If a client has worked with multiple professionals in a firm, it becomes very difficult for a single professional to influence them or entice them to follow.

- Remove or "disguise" revenue ownership in the compensation model—It might be impractical and undesirable to remove completely the revenue under management as a component of compensation (in fact, I advocated for it several times in the compensations section), but you may try to disguise or mitigate the connection by adding multiple other measures.
- Show no tolerance for language that implies individual ownership—If professionals use language such as "my client" it will be very difficult for them not to act as if the client is literally "theirs." Language has special power—we tend to believe what we say, and things we say often tend to become real. Have you ever tried to read the word "red" if the word itself is written in green ink? It is extremely difficult to do so.[1]
- Have the partners set an example—If partners are sharing their client relationships with each other and with other professionals in the firm, everyone is much more likely to do the same. In a similar fashion, if you say "our client" every day it will be very difficult for your mind to maintain that you actually own the client.

## Mom and Dad

My little daughter is six years old, and she does something that every child her age does—test mom and dad. She will come to me and ask if she can have some candy before dinner. I will say "no" and might even try to explain the nutritional logic of skipping the chocolates. My daughter will say "Okay," and then go straight to my wife and ask the same question—"Can I have some candy?"

In a firm with multiple partners, you will each have influence over employees, and your behavior and statements will be observed by the staff. Any discrepancy will be noted and will create potential confusion, friction, or even conflict. It is extremely difficult for employees to function in an environment where the partners hold conflicting values. This does not mean that the partners are in conflict with each other—not at all. It simply means that the two (or 20) of you have differing values and that you need to help employees reconcile those values.

For example, one partner may be the "idea guy" and highly value innovation and intellectual contribution. Another partner may be more of the "process guy" and highly value process, error-free execution, and attention to detail. You can't really be very creating and error-free at the same time, so it might be difficult for employees to figure out which they should be. It is also common for one partner to value sales and business development very highly while the other is focused on operations and feels some resentment for sales "offering things we can't do." Once again, that is confusing and at times dysfunctional.

Some discrepancy is normal and natural and is quite acceptable. However, when there are major differences in values that potentially conflict, the partners need to find a way to reconcile such differences and appear in front of employees with a consolidated front. The worst-case scenario is to wage battles against each other using the employees as pawns. Unfortunately, this often happens. You hear statements such as "Mark may think otherwise but I tell you, this firm runs on. . . ." This is just dysfunctional and over time will create issues between the partners and the employees.

## Tribes

There are times when the issue of divergence between the partners becomes a fundamental difference between groups in the firm where two or more subcultures emerge. Almost like tribes, the departments and/or offices (the most common sources of tribal division) start identifying themselves as different and distinct from the other group. Quickly that escalates into a self-fulfilling prophecy and the groups really do become very different.

If it's not too late, you should try to stop that process before it gains momentum. Tribal mentality results in friction, conflict, inefficiency, and aggravation and can waste the vital emotional energy of the group on in-fighting instead of building the business. Unfortunately, it is a rather natural instinct for people. There are even experiments where teenage boys at a camp were split into two different buildings[2] and then asked to describe the kids in the other buildings. Predictably so, they started creating a stereotype for the boys in the other buildings and identifying themselves as members of their own building—an identity separate and distinct from the others. Think of Harry Potter and his Gryffindor friends.

The only way to prevent such behavior is to encourage the groups to interact with each other and tackle challenges together in mixed teams rather than in isolation. This means that insisting on staff meetings being attended by everyone, discouraging clique-y social events, creating cross-functional teams, and other such initiatives is critical for avoiding the tribes. This issue is particularly exacerbated in firms with multiple locations since the lack of daily contact can create even further isolation. Similarly, when there are distinct teams working with each partner, there should be extra attention given to preventing the teams identifying themselves as "John's team."

## Manage Yourself

"How can you manage others if you can't manage yourself," asked Peter Drucker,[3] perhaps the most respected management scientist of all times. Being a business leader requires an extraordinary level of focus, self-discipline, and most of all self-awareness. This constant awareness of your strengths, weaknesses, and interests is particularly challenging and taxing. After all, as the "captain of this ship" you are supposed to somehow have an unwavering conviction of the success of the journey while at the same time maintaining a very clear view of the fact that you may be completely and totally wrong.

Managing stress is perhaps the most difficult aspect of maintaining your composure and steadfast sense of direction. Stress wears us out, day after day, and as business owners we are only human. We have all had the moment when we wished we could tell everybody (clients and employees), "Just leave me alone for a moment; let me deal with my life for a day." It is very difficult to resist that reaction, and I have struggled and continue to struggle with that aspect of leadership. I have no answers for you, dear reader—it is just tough!

That said, Valerie Brown, CEO of Cetera, suggested a course in mindful leadership—a meditation practice adapted for business leaders—as a good way to tackle that problem, and I can't thank her enough for that suggestion. After a five-day course in mindfulness, I try to meditate daily for 20 minutes, and I find that the days when I meditate are much different and much better than the days I don't. Meditation won't suddenly turn you into a New Age, Buddhist hippie. Instead, it will help you clear your mind, focus it on the moment, and perhaps pause for one extra second before you respond to what business throws at you. Respond, rather than react is a key of what I learned from the course and it has been one of the best lessons I have ever learned.

Culture is what happens when no one is watching, and you will find that the more the firm grows, the more things happen while you are not there to see them. The good news is that the firm is very likely to behave like you, the owner, do. Unfortunately, that's the bad news—you may see things you don't like only to recognize your own mirror image. That's why self-awareness and the ability to discipline yourself often makes the difference between a great advisor and a great CEO.

## Notes

1. This is known as the Stroop effect after John Ridley Stroop, who described the effect in "Studies of Interference in Serial Verbal Reaction," *Journal of Experimental Psychology*, 1935.
2. This experiment is known as the Robbers Cave Experiment. Muzafer and Carolyn Sherif conducted the experiment in Robbers Cave Park in Oklahoma in 1954 and published the results in *The Robbers Cave Experiment: Intergroup Conflict and Cooperation*, by Muzafer Sherif, O. J. Harvey, B. Jack White, William R. Hood, and Carolyn W. Sherif (1954/1961).
3. Peter Drucker, "Managing Oneself, *Best of HBR*, 1999.

# CHAPTER 8

# Making Partner

An ownership track ("partner track") is perhaps the clearest expression of the values of a firm. Nothing reflects as clearly and as truly what is important and valued in a firm than the criteria for the ultimate prize—becoming an owner. The decision to promote the first partner internally is perhaps the biggest achievement of an ensemble firm. There is no better way to signify the importance of working together as one firm than sharing the profits and equity of the firm with some of its best people. How and when you do it makes a very strong statement about the nature of your organization. Having a partnership track is perhaps the strongest motivator available for the top performers in your firm.

The partnership track we will explore in this chapter relies on two fundamental principles. The first is that being an owner is a privilege reserved for only the very best and most accomplished people in the firm. It is a privilege that takes a long time to earn and represents a very strong commitment from both parties (the firm and the partner candidate). The second principle is that partners are selected not just based on economic logic but that they also have to demonstrate the character and behavior expected of a partner. In other words, that bringing clients to the firm or being an outstanding investment manager is not enough in itself to earn a partner role; professionals also need to show their maturity in decision making and ethical judgment in their work.

These seem like very lofty statements; after all, we are not talking about someone becoming the controlling shareholder of the firm. They are most likely going to be a 1 percent to 10 percent owner. Why do we set such high expectations? The answer is that making someone a partner in a business is very difficult to undo, and it also allows them to represent the firm through their actions. Think of making someone your partner as teaching someone

121

to perfectly mimic your signature so that no one can tell the difference. Think of the power this person will have—they can sign contracts that commit you to long-term obligations, they can sign checks from your checkbook, they can send letters to your employees on your behalf. Well . . . that pretty much describes your partner.

Many firms look at promoting a partner as a strictly economic decision, that is, if they bring enough business they get to be a partner. I would propose that we look at a number of noneconomic criteria as well. However, before we create the criteria for who should be a partner, we need to first ask if the firm is ready for more partners. Similarly, there is a tendency to rush to the discussion of how the new partners will buy-in or how the purchase will be financed. Instead, I propose a different sequence of decisions: (1) When is the firm ready for another partner? (2) What are the criteria for new partners? (3) How do we measure and communicate the criteria? And then last, (4) How do they buy-in?

## When Can You Add a Partner?

I believe most owners would agree that unless the firm grows substantially, adding more partners will only result in diluting the income and equity of existing partners. Adding more partners is fundamentally premised on the notion that owning, say, 95 percent of a bigger firm is better than having 100 percent of a smaller firm. Determining how much bigger the firm has to be before that statement is true is the first step.

Mathematically, it is pretty easy to determine how much bigger the firm should be to prevent reduction of the income of existing owners. For example, let's say that the existing owners have determined that they will offer a 5 percent ownership to one of the advisors and that their current income is $1 million. This means that after the new partner admission 95 percent of the income still has to equal $1 million, or $1 million divided by 95 percent = $1,052,632. So the firm has to add about $52,000 in income—round it up to $60,000 before it can add a 5 percent owner. If the firm has a profit margin of 25 percent, then the firm has to add about $240,000 in new revenue ($60,000 divided by 25 percent).

Of course, in most cases the partner promotion will also result in some increase in base compensation as well as some other benefits and perks. The value of such compensation increases should be added to the income number. Let's assume, for example, that new partners get a "bump" in their base compensation of $30,000 and also a package of perks and benefits worth $10,000. This means that the firm needs as much as $100,000 in new income to avoid reduction in existing partner income ($60,000 in income, $30,000 in base compensation, and $10,000 in perks). This increase in income will require $400,000 in new revenue ($100,000 divided by 25 percent).

This may not seem like a very intimidating number, but put yourself in the shoes of an owner and think of it this way: The next $400,000 in new revenue are not going to add anything to your income—not a single cent. Think of how long the firm may take to grow by $400,000—could be a couple of years or more. Can you accept such a long period without any growth to your income? This mathematical approach may be over-simplifying things, but in fact, large partnerships often set a target for partner income and derive their partnership admissions from that target. For example, accounting firms sometimes look to drive average partner income to, say, $400,000 (inclusive of base compensation and distributions). Given a normal expense ratio before compensation to the partners of, say, 60 percent, this suggest that every partner should be managing around $1 million in revenue, since 40 percent (100 percent less expenses of 60 percent) of this revenue equals the target income of $400,000. So roughly for every $1 million the firm should add another partner.

The other approach to looking at the growth of the firm is more focused on "span of control"—how many clients and revenues an owner can manage and oversee. Assuming that having revenues and clients beyond the "span of control" of a partner are at risk of leaving the firm or receiving poor service, the firm is better off promoting a partner to take care of those clients. As crude as this example can be, think of clients or AUM as sheep and consider that partners are shepherds. For every 200 sheep, for example, you may want to have one shepherd, and when you exhaust the capacity of existing shepherds, you need to add another one or you will start losing sheep.

Finally, many firms simply look for growth in the revenues of the firm in the last two to three years and then cross-reference that with the individuals who are ready to step up to the ownership level. The theory here is that as long as you have a good candidate and as long as you have the confidence that the firm is growing well, you don't want to keep that person waiting for too long.

For practical purposes, I have seen most of the firms I have worked with combine the growth criteria with the availability of candidates. Especially in the growth spur between 2003 and 2007, firms were quite aggressive in promoting new partners with the confidence that the growth would be there. The crisis of 2008 and 2009 put a stop on all partner promotions and put many careers on hold. As firms started growing again, they needed in some cases to make the promotions despite not reaching the exact growth targets since the candidates had been waiting for a while.

As a rule of thumb, I propose to the firms that I have worked with that they should look to add a partner for every $750,000 to $1 million in revenue. If they are adding partners at a rate of faster than $750,000 in revenue, they are risking diluting income of the existing partners. If they are waiting much past $1 million in revenue per partner, they are risking some span of control issues.

## Whom Do You Want as a Partner?

The criteria of who should be a partner should cover the character and total performance of the candidate and not just his or her revenue contribution. The criteria should never be formulaic, and there is very little reason I can see for not publishing the criteria to all employees. After all, if you want the partner promotion to motivate, you have to establish what the rules are for earning it are. That said, it should also be clear that the existing partners are "judge and jury" on how those criteria are applied to a candidate. I remember how I felt as a candidate for partner in Moss Adams; I really wished the criteria were clearer—as in a formula. On the other hand, as soon as I became an owner, I immediately realized the merit of broader and evaluation-based measures. This is very typical—partner candidates have to remember that one day they will be "on the inside" evaluating those who are trying to join the ownership group.

The criteria for partner admission should be very individual for every firm, but most firms will be focusing on the following categories:

1. Revenue contribution.
2. Management contribution.
3. Character.
4. Community and market presence and representing the firm.
5. Intellectual contribution.

I remember listening to a presentation by Bob Bunting, the long-time chairman and leader of Moss Adams, in which he was saying that each partner in the firm should have four critical skills: business development, client service, people management, and compliance. His thesis was that the firm cannot have partners that are missing one of those skills because this will create critical weaknesses and potential problems. Not all partners have to be great in every single area, but they have to be at least good in each. This list of criteria below is essentially a modification of the same notion.

## Revenue Contribution

Revenue contribution receives the most attention since it is the easiest to measure and is directly linked to growth of the firm. Typically the contribution of a candidate can be expressed in the revenue they have personally added, and most firms will be tracking that number in their normal course of business. Also, some firms measure the additional business a candidate has generated from existing clients. This "internal" business development is usually considered part of the "business brought" and in most cases is treated as equally valuable.

Another measure that firms can use is the revenue managed by the candidate as a lead advisor. This will be revenue from clients that see the advisor as their primary relationship with the firm, regardless of who originated the relationship. Thus if an advisor has, for example, $500,000 in revenue from clients that the firm has assigned to her and she is managing all of those relationships as the primary advisor, then all $500,000 will be considered part of her "contribution."

Not every firm agrees that revenue management is as valuable as the addition of new clients. In general, firms that have a solid track record of growth and access to institutional sources of leads such as accounting firms or banks tend to value revenue management as high as sales. Firms that have had a harder time growing and that rely more on individual effort and marketing for growth tend to discount revenue management as a criterion.

My advice is to not go too far to either extreme. I don't believe a firm can have a sustainable future without every partner having contributed at least some significant amount of new revenue to the firm. If some of the partners have never brought a client to the firm, the firm will be very vulnerable to the loss of its business developers. This often happens to firms where the first generation are the true business developers and the second generation of partners have always received clients from the firm. What happens frequently in such cases is that the first generation realizes that if they retire, the future of the firm is very uncertain despite the fact that they supposedly have many partners. The result is that they often sell externally to reduce the risk.

On the other hand, if a firm does not value revenue management, it is really undermining the most crucial aspect of firm success—client retention. Most referrals come from existing clients, and therefore client retention and satisfaction is the key to successful business development. Undervaluing client retention in favor of sales can create the atmosphere of a brokerage boiler room, and most wealth management firms would rather avoid that.

## Management Contribution

The very concept of an ensemble firm requires working as a team. Advisors who are good team managers and are skilled at developing people deserve significant credit for that contribution. That said, every partner needs to take a role in managing the firm and its employees, and a firm really can't afford to have too many partners who are "not good at managing." This creates the wrong atmosphere and sends the wrong message.

Testing the management skills of the partner candidates requires consistently giving them management responsibilities; not just one project. The last two or three years before making partner should be a time when the candidates consistently participate in management. This should involve responsibility for supervising employees and training other associates. It should also include the management of a larger scale project such as converting to a new system, changing pricing, implementing a new workflow, and so on.

## Character

Evaluating character is a very subjective task but that should not stop firms from expressing their expectations for new partners and actually evaluating how the candidates compare to those expectations. It may sound a little corny to have the partners meet and consider whether someone exhibits integrity, sound judgment, high ethical standards, and so forth but at the end of the day, character is the difference between a partner who will get the entire firm in trouble and someone who will elevate it to new heights.

As much as the category is subjective, there are many criteria that are objective and can be applied in this process. This includes credit third party references and feedback from the employees the candidate has worked with. Perhaps the firm can also consider the typical employee screening tools such as credit checks and background checks. It is a somewhat touchy subject whether the firm should stand in the way of someone making partner because of a poor credit record or transgressions in college. At the same time you always have to ask yourself, whom do I want to call my partner? Are you comfortable saying, my partner just declared bankruptcy? Can you say, my partner was arrested for drunken driving? Partnerships are very personal and very close relationships. You are not making a decision about who should be allowed in your condo building. You are making the decision about who can ruin or improve your business.

## Presence

Community presence and reputation is tied to business development. While not forced, such presence should be encouraged as it will serve as the foundation for future lead-generation and will raise the reputation of the firm. Activities that elevate the profile and reputation of the firm should be heavily encouraged. This includes professional organizations, local organizations that are relevant to the firm's business, and charitable boards. The focus here is whether or not having this partner on board makes the firm better known and highly regarded.

## Intellectual Contribution

Financial planning, investment advice, and investment management are intellectual pursuits by nature, and each professional will be making an intellectual contribution to the firm by simply practicing. That said, some forms of intellectual contribution turn into a competitive advantage for the firm. For example: enhanced planning methods and processes, proprietary research, unique investment models, and so on. The professionals who make such extraordinary contributions deserve special consideration for partnership. Think of them as the "scientists" in the firm. At times valuing their revenue contribution may be more difficult since they are focused heavily on internal processes. However, what they add in the form of intellectual capital should not be ignored.

## Is Partnership Only for Advisors?

Partnership opportunities should not be restricted only to advisors. A successful firm is impossible without strong leadership in the operations functions of the firm. All of the qualities and criteria we have described so far apply to operations managers as well. The only factor that is not so directly applicable is the revenue contribution. The requirement to grow the firm to a certain level of revenue for each partner may make it more difficult for operations staff to be considered. Still, every firm should look at its operations leaders and determine if it is able to offer them ownership. In particular, positions such as (if full time) chief operations officer, chief compliance officer, and chief financial officer are all strong candidates for ownership in a super-ensemble firm.

## How Do They Buy-In?

First of all, it should be understood that new partners will buy their shares rather than have them "granted." Granting shares completely undermines the value of the firm and also creates a dangerous precedent. I was listening to a presentation by the manager of one of the giant resorts in Las Vegas who was explaining that contrary to popular perception, their resort does not discount the hotel rooms in order to attract gamblers. His logic was ironclad: "You can't expect people who pay $100 for their room to gamble at a $5,000/minimum table or pay $500 for dinner." Very much the same is true for incoming partners; you can't expect the same partners who paid nothing for their first shares to someday buy you out at three times the revenue.

It is natural for the senior partners to feel sympathy and loyalty for their associates and try to give them favorable terms on the buy-in. The right place for expressing that sympathy is by providing financing rather than severely discounting the valuation of the firm or even giving part of it for free.

The term "sweat equity" typically applies to situations where somebody was severely overpaid for years while the firm was being built not an employee who has been with the firm but has been well paid for his or her work. Employees who have worked at market-level compensation, in my mind, would not have sweat equity or have the right to some "grant" or "discount." Only in cases where an employee was underpaid or his or her contribution to the firm was well beyond the expectation for the position, a sweat equity package may be applicable. In such cases it is good to quantify the extent of the underpayment in compensation and try to translate that into a purchase of comparable value.

For example, an exception can be made for a lead advisor who for years accepted a salary of $50,000 rather than the more typical $100,000 or more. The extent of underpayment was $50,000 per year. Or an investment manager who for years managed the assets of the firm and created the performance track record that gave the firm its reputation today. However "sweat equity" will not apply to an employee advisor who had a salary of $90,000 but thought he or she could have earned $120,000 in another firm.

## Valuation

There are two methods used in the valuation of advisory firms for internal transactions. The most common method is to establish a formula such as a multiple of earnings (better) or revenue. Such formulas are common knowledge and are frequently discussed in industry reports and publications.

The alternative method is to hire an expert valuation firm to perform an appraisal of the firm.

We have discussed the merits of the two methods in the chapter on mergers, but we should cover those quickly in this context.

- Multiples should be applied with caution since they are easy to misuse. Most of all, you should make sure that you are using the right numbers from a good source, for example, research reports or M&A experts. Second, you should make sure that you are using multiples from firms of similar size. It is easy to get carried away by the high multiples paid for super-ensembles in consolidation deals. The multiple you use should originate from firms of similar size.
- If the firm has high expenses and therefore lower profitability than the industry benchmarks, it will be quite dangerous to use revenue multiples. Revenue multiples imply a certain level of normal profitability. If the profit is not there, the income derived from the purchase will not be enough to complete the purchase. For example, if a firm has only 10 percent profit margin with profits of $1 million and is valued at 2.5 times revenue of $10 million, a 5 percent stake in the firm will be valued at 5 percent × 2.5 × $10,000,000 = $1,250,000. An astounding sum, considering that it only generates $50,000 in income. With an interest rate of 5 percent, it will take somebody approximately 17 years to complete the buy-in if they use the dividend as the primary source of cash for the payment.
- Professional valuations, when done well, are a very objective and balanced view of the practice. However, you have to make sure that the appraiser understands your firm and your economics well—how fast are you growing, what are your clients like, what is the operational and service process? If they are not asking these questions (and many others), you may not be working with the right firm.

No matter what the valuation method, the valuation usually yields what is known as "enterprise value"—the value of the entire firm if purchased as one whole. There are a number of studies suggesting that one share in a minority interest of a shareholder is worth less than a share in a controlling interest. Studies suggest that this minority interest discount may be as much as 33 percent.[1] Deciding whether or not to apply this discount is difficult; on one hand, the founder often holds a majority share and is hurting his or her own interest by "retailing" it. This is sort of like selling your house one room at a time. On the other hand, the new partners clearly are not going to have the benefit of control. Usually, this conundrum is resolved by offering very favorable financing terms and perhaps using less aggressive valuation assumptions.

## Financing

In nine out of 10 cases that I have observed of firms promoting partners internally, the firm has financed the purchase. Almost by definition the new partners are full of energy, ambition, and drive and quite devoid of the financial resources to purchase shares from their firm. The only times when I have seen new partners making an outright purchase have been cases where this is the second career for the new partners and they have enjoyed significant success in their prior career. Of course, having rich parents or a rich spouse is always a plus. However, choosing your partners based on their ability to buy-in is a recipe for disaster.

In most cases the firm will supply a five- to eight-year loan for the purchase. Usually the terms of the loan are engineered in such a way that the new partner can keep his or her base compensation (or most of it) and use "bonuses" or dividend distributions for the buy-in. For example, if the firm has $500,000 in profits (real profits after partner salaries) and was valued at $3 million, and a new partner purchased a 5 percent share valued at $150,000 (5 percent × $3 million valuation), the new partner's pretax distributions will be $25,000 and the after-tax distribution will be around (very rough approximation) $18,000. At 5 percent interest, it will take the new partner between seven and eight years to buy in to the full $150,000, assuming no changes in the firm's profitability. Of course, everyone is hoping that the firm profits will continue to grow so that the partner can buy-in faster or use some of the extra money for a Lexus or BMW (the two official cars of "making partner"). I have also seen schedules that have balloon payments or increasing payments over time, essentially allowing the new partner to "taste" some of the extra cash early on.

It is also not unusual to see some vesting provisions such as forfeiting of all shares if there is a default on the buy-in or if the new partner leaves before the buy-in is complete. The partner may also not be able to vote until completing the buy-in.

Many firms prefer to seek external financing for the buy-in, and there is a solid logic behind it. After all, who wants to be the "bad guy" and collect those payments from a young partner who is buying in? There may also be some emotional decisions to make at some point. What if the market declines and the income of the partner declines? Will the person be allowed to renegotiate the loan? A bank may handle such issues more impersonally and without causing friction in the partnership. However, realistically, there are not many banks that will lend at this size of contract and without collateral (shares in a small practice are not the kind of collateral most banks seek). As a result, you should almost expect that you will have to finance the purchase.

## Alternatives to Full Partnership

There are many alternatives to the sale of shares or units to a new partner, and all of those alternatives have purpose and merit. However, it should be understood that all alternatives are not nearly as powerful as motivators as full ownership. The idea of "making partner" is a badge of honor, a sign of achievement, and a status symbol that goes well beyond the monetary effect of the dividend or equity accumulation. After all, for most new partners their income and wealth will barely change beyond a few percentages. Why is it that most young professionals dedicate so many years of effort to this rather small reward? The answer lies in the psychological effect of being an owner in the firm, and that effect cannot be replicated by the synthetic equity options.

No one puts on their business card "Philip Palaveev—Phantom Stock Owner." No one calls their mom to say, "Mom, I just got stock appreciation rights!"[2] Professionals want to be able to say, "I made partner!" My actual title in Moss Adams was "principal" due to regulations governing the ownership of CPA firms by non-CPAs (I am not a CPA). I don't think I ever used that title in either casual or official conversation. "Partner" is what I wanted to be called.

If ownership has three components—income, control, and appreciation (equity value), then the easiest way of thinking of the partnership alternatives is that they strip one or two of the three components. Income partnerships provide income but no vote or equity value; phantom stock and stock appreciation rights provide equity but no voting or income. The same is true for stock options before they are exercised.

All of these alternatives have tax and legal implications, which I am not qualified to discuss, but if you have an interest in implementing one of these options, you will need to work closely with your attorney and CPA.

## Income Partnerships

Income partnerships are very popular among law firms, and advisors are understandably interested in the idea of sharing profits with a key employee but not sharing voting power or equity appreciation. Most advisors are pathological owners—they want to own and control, and it is much easier for them to share profits than to share the equity. The setup of an income partnership is pretty straightforward and so are the advantages and disadvantages. On the plus side for candidates, they won't have to buy in and go through years of payments. Realistically, a small share of the firm does not give them any control anyway, so the only thing they are missing is the equity appreciation. On the negative side, this is barely more than a bonus plan, and it is hard not to feel that you "not quite an owner." In addition, all the income generated will be regular income for tax purposes, without the benefit of a future capital gains tax event.

## Phantom Stock, Stock Appreciation Rights, and Stock Options

If income partnerships generate income without the ability to vote or participate in the appreciation of a firm, the synthetic stock instruments allow participating in the appreciation but do not generate income or allow the recipient to vote.

Phantom stock allows the recipient to participate in a percentage of the proceeds from the sale of the company—for example, 10 percent. Unless the company is sold or otherwise liquidated, the recipient will not see any benefit from the phantom shares. However, if the company goes through a transaction, then they become quite valuable. Different arrangements can be made to differentiate between "a transaction" as in any sale of stock or "a change of control transaction." Since they are only valuable upon a sale, they are most often used with companies that are very likely to sell. For example, an aging owner group that has not made succession plans and therefore is facing some nervousness from the key employees might see this as a good way to quell the fears.

Stock appreciation rights (SAR) work in a very similar way, but rather than relying on a transaction, they rely on a valuation. So a recipient might get a package of, say, 100,000 units valued at $1 each based on the current valuation of the firm. The package will typically specify a subsequent valuation, for example, in five years. If at the time the units are worth $2 each, then the SAR recipient will get $100,000 ($2/unit × 100,000 units less the base price of $1/unit × 100,000 units).

The fact that SARs pay without an equity event makes them much more attractive and valuable to the employee. As long as the company appreciates, he or she doesn't have to wait for the company to be sold. Unfortunately, that's the major drawback for the company—the SARs will generate a very substantial cash liability without the liquidity (sale) to meet it. Such instruments are usually used by cash-rich companies that do not want to expand ownership but need to tie in key managers.

Stock options were made very popular by the dot-com entrepreneurs and for a good reason—they are perfect for a company that intends to go public or have a liquidity event. Much like SARs, options have a "strike price" on the company shares and allow the employee to purchase shares at that price at a future date. So say the package is for 100,000 shares at $1/share, and the company goes public at $15/share three years from now when the options mature. The employee can purchase the shares at $1 and then immediately sell them at $15/share, generating $14/share profit $\times$ 100,000 = $1,400,000 (house in Hawaii, here we come!). Unfortunately for advisors, that second transaction is the hitch—unless the company has a liquidity event planned, the employee will either have to hold the shares and become a real owner OR sell the shares to the company at a set valuation.

Some advisory firms have played with options as a way of locking in a low price for future partners—an interesting idea. Others have provided "cashless exercise" to employees (essentially the same mechanism as an SAR). However, I can't say that I have seen stock options used much by advisors.

## Profits Interest

While I admit to dismissing the synthetic equity options as very limited in their power to motivate, I should point out that profits interest is a method for adding partners that deserves special consideration. The idea of profits interest is that the value and income built by the partner(s) year to date remains their own but that the growth in income and value will be shared with the new partner. For example, assume a firm has $1 million in income and $6 million in value. A typical profits interest agreement will be for the incoming partner to receive, say, 10 percent of the growth in income over the first $1 million and 10 percent of the value beyond the first $6 million.

Suppose that in five years the firm has $2 million in income and $12 million in value. The partner who received the profits interest will have a claim to 10 percent of $2 million less $1 million (belonging to the founders) = $100,000 (10 percent $\times$ ($2,000,000 − $1,000,000)). Similarly, she will have a claim to 10 percent of the $6 million in appreciation since she became a partner (10% $\times$ ($12,000,000 − $6,000,000) = $600,000.

The elegance of this solution is the fact that at the time of the agreement, the agreement has no value—it only becomes valuable if the firm grows and appreciates. This means that new partners can start calling themselves owners, but they really have no ownership and thus need not pay any cash. This "cash-free" ownership is very attractive and removes the need for all the financing discussions. What is more, the founders do not fear dilution since by definition, if the firm does not grow, there is no sharing of income or equity.

Profits interest arrangements come at a price, though—first, the appreciation and accumulation of ownership will be rather slow compared to other methods. For example, if someone has a 10 percent interest in the growth of a firm and the firm grows in income and value by 20 percent, then he or she becomes the owner of 10 percent of the 120 percent or 1.2 percent. Twenty percent is a very strong year and 1.2 percent is not a very large number.

The second issue with the profits interest is that that the ownership can be completely "wiped out" if the revenue and profit declines. For example, I was a profit interest partner in Fusion in 2008 when the revenue declined by about 20 percent. I started the year with high expectations and ended it with exactly 0 percent ownership. It took about a year and a half for the value to recover. Profits interest owners may also be very opposed to any equity transactions in the early years of their agreement for the same reason.

Finally, it is difficult to use this method for partner admission more than once or twice. If you admit six or seven partners this way, you will have a cascading number of thresholds for each partner and a very difficult time understanding who owns how much. Even with one such agreement, you will have to call your CPA every time you need to know who has what percentage of the firm.

With those issues in mind, the profits interest is a great way of adding new partners without straining them with loan payments. It also ties the interest of the new partners to growth, which is exactly what the "old partners" aim for.

## Why Do You Promote Partners?

Whichever method of partner promotion you choose to use and however you value your firm and finance the transaction, you have to remember why you are doing this. The reasons are many—reward and retain your best people, motivate your key employees to exercise the care and caution of an owner, drive your advisors to grow the firm with you, reduce dependence on the owner(s), create multiple options for exit and succession, allow yourself more time off since others will cover for you, strengthen the management team by adding more owners with unique skills and experience. Hopefully your motivation comes from one of these reasons. There are also many ways in which I have seen firms get disappointed by the new partners. You won't be able to cash out some money, create a buy-out for yourself, increase your valuation, not have to manage the firm anymore, find somebody else to come in to work on the weekends. If the goal is right, the path will be right too—in other words, if you are adding partners for the right reasons, the mechanics of that addition tend to work out well.

## Notes

1. Z. Christopher Mercer, "A Brief Review of Control Premiums and Minority Interest Discounts," *The Journal of Business Valuation*, 2011.
2. "Oh my god! Is that contagious?" is a very likely answer.

# CHAPTER 9

# The Big Idea

We have discussed at length the advantages of the ensemble firm model—ensemble financial advisory firms are more profitable, grow faster, and have higher equity value per dollar of profit. They also have an advantage in attracting talent and have an easier time establishing referral relationships Yet, why do so very few firms manage to reach the size and scale where they can reach these advantages? The answer lies in the ability of advisory firms to formulate a firm identity that does not rely on specific individual reputation—a "big idea" that can unite the firm and brand it in the market.

## Four Stages of Growth

The biggest obstacle to growth that otherwise successful firms face is the ability to define and deliver a value proposition that goes beyond the skills and expertise of the original owner or a small group of owners. "Trapped" in the physical limitation of time, energy, and knowledge that the principals (owners) possess, firms struggle to create a business model that can transcend that limitation and allow them to reach the true advantages of size—most of all market dominance, reputation, and ability to add talent.

Consider this:

- The 2010 Advisor One Survey[1] of the top wealth managers in the country shows that firms with over $1 billion in AUM had consistently higher growth rates every year since 2005 compared to their smaller competitors. The billion-dollar firms in the survey also showed higher revenue per client and higher productivity ratios.

- The Fusion Challenge Survey[2] shows that the largest firms had close to three times higher income per owner ($935,000) compared to their smaller peers ($338,000).
- The "Real Deals" report published by Pershing LLC and FA Insight[3] shows valuation ratios of three times revenue and higher for the largest firms, compared to the ratios reported for smaller practices in the FP Transition reports (ratios range from 2.2 × revenue to 2.5 × revenue).

Growing past the owners, however, is very difficult for most firms—it is counterintuitive to the owners, often culturally objectionable as it violates the values of the firm, and frequently it is even undesirable to the professionals in the firm as it runs contrary to their personal definition of success. Yet, for firms that aspire to achieve dominant size and the strategic position that comes with it, there is a reliable path of transformation that can be followed. The path requires emphasis on strategy and process, perhaps at the expense of individualized attention to professional careers.

If we trace the evolution of an advisory firm from origin to the largest size category (let's assume a large firm is one with over $1 billion in AUM), we can define the growth in these four stages:

1. Practice Growth—One or more owners are trying to grow their practice to critical size. The focus is on acquiring clients. The value proposition focuses on the attention and time the owners will devote to their clients. The acquisition of clients is often unselective and opportunistic. There is little focus on business management as the owners are the business. Revenues can range from $500,000 to $1 million before the practice has to enter the next stage.
2. Team Service—Having grown to critical mass and met basic income requirements, the practice starts to focus on adding staff. Employees are hired for specific functions, and they start playing significant roles in client service. Positions such as client service administrator and associate advisor are added. While the value proposition still rests with the skills of the owners, the service delivery is based on a team. The firm starts to consider its strategy and add clients selectively. There is emphasis on employee training, compensation, and management. Revenues can range from $1 million to $3 million in this stage, depending on the number of partners.
3. Partnership—The firm starts to use employee professionals—nonowner employees who independently service clients. There are protocols and standards for service that are established and followed throughout the

practice. Employee management practices are well developed and thought out. The strategy of the firm is well articulated, and there is a systematic business development process. Client selection and risk management are emphasized, and the partners of the firm act as a management team. Revenues range from $3 million to $10 million at this stage.

4. Past the Owners (Institutionalizing)—The firm has developed a value proposition that is abstract and institutional in nature. The owners are recognizable, but not essential to the value proposition of the firm or delivery of service. The firm has a strong sense of identity that is shared by the entire professional team. Owners focus their time on strategic-level projects. Ownership and firm management become separated—some owners focus on management only—and departments within the firm are clearly defined. The culture of the firm is no longer defined or controlled by the owners. Revenues exceed $10 million.

The fourth phase defies many otherwise successful firms and continues to be a challenge for all successful firms. Even among the top firms in the industry, if we were to interview the clients and the staff of the firm, we would find that they think of the firm as "Bob's firm." Similarly, the value proposition of the firm boils down to "you get to work with Bob"— Bob being working title for the owner/principal/lead advisor of the firm. It is really Bob's expertise and knowledge that the client is attracted to and wants to associate with. Bob's ability to communicate and respond to the client will further become part of the value proposition. You will hear clients and staff describing the firm as "Bob's firm" and chances are the same description is used by many referral sources. Chances are Bob thinks of the firm in those terms too. We could call this value proposition the "rent-the-owner" proposition. Over time, as the firm grows it may become "Bob and Scott's firm" or even "Bob, Scott, and Stu," but the firm is completely defined by two or three names. This owner-dependent proposition is natural and inevitable in the "Practice Growth" and "Team Service" stage, but starts to get in the way in the "Partnership" stage and becomes a barrier to entering the largest stage of growth.

A firm can grow very large on the strength of the expertise and talents of the owners. The rent-the-owner strategy is very appealing and intuitive, but ultimately flawed. It is easy to deploy and comes to the owners naturally. It is also easy for clients to understand—people easily relate to other people and develop personal relationships. It is much more difficult to win their allegiance to an idea or a concept. The flaw in this approach, though, is that ultimately it relies on "Bob"—when Bob is gone, the firm will have to somehow find "new Bob" to replace him. It is hard to create high equity value in this model, and it is hard to grow the firm past the individual limitations of "Bob and partners." Those limitations can be simply time available, but they can also be skills, expertise, aptitude to tackle certain kinds of business, and so forth. Ultimately, "Bob's firm" will have to reinvent itself as "Your Name's firm" and is always at risk of entering a cycle of slower growth and declining opportunity, usually as "Bob" chooses to slow down himself.

## Steps to Institutionalizing

The rent-the-owner proposition is difficult to change or overcome, but for those firms who aspire to become multibillion-dollar enterprises with lasting presence, changing the model to an institutionalized value proposition is essential. The firms that I have worked with that have been successful in this transition tend to follow these eight steps:

1. **Conceptualize an institutional value proposition and structure your strategy and business plans around it.** Before building the institutional firm, you have to be able to draw the blueprint—the conceptual value proposition you are trying to implement. How can you differentiate as a firm, as opposed to individually? What are the components of your personal expertise and experience that are transferable to the firm?

   Examples of institutionalized strategies are firms that focus on specific target markets and develop unique tools that service that market—for example, Mercer Global Advisors and the way they specialize in servicing dentists. Note the difference here between a strategy that can be institutionalized and a similar strategy that still relies on the owners. There are many firms that have one partner who knows something about dentists. Mercer, however, has built its entire business model and expertise around that market.

   In developing the concept, you need to focus on differentiating factors that can be institutionalized. The incomplete list of such factors includes data and the insight from it, in-depth knowledge of a distinct market niche, methods for training and developing staff, unique investment style and models, a service culture that can propagate itself in multiple locations, and so on. Just as with a house, if you can't draw it first, you shouldn't start building it.

2. **Structure client service around repeatable steps that can be accomplished by trained employees with the kind of skills that are widely available in the market.** Most institutional strategies require the creation

of a repeatable service experience that the firm can train to. While it is certainly possible to become the kind of firm that develops a custom process and hires the brightest people to figure out each individual case (e.g., the consulting firm McKinsey), most firms focus on strategies that favor service standardization. The repeatable process will allow the firm to hire widely available talent and employ them in delivering extraordinary service.

Without a clearly understood service process, junior professional positions will struggle to match the expectations of the client or replicate what "Bob" can do. That frustration is usually visible among both the professionals and the clients they service—there is a sense of downgrading if they don't work with Bob. This becomes a severe capacity limitation (Bob is the scarce resource) and tends to promote a culture of "wanting to be Bob." Needless to say, when the professionals finally acquire the skills and expertise to be like Bob, they tend to look for a position inside or outside of the firm that gives them the control and power "Bob" had—that is, they either fracture the firm by building their own little silo or leave to start one of their own.

3. **Identify markets and sources of new business that support the institutional value proposition and find business development processes that are consistent with the strategy.** Not every market will support an institutionalized approach. In fact, I would propose that the best markets for an institutionalized firm are at the two extremes of the wealth spectrum—the mass market and the very high net worth. The reason is that they have service expectations that are consistent with the idea of a firm-level service. The small, mass market accounts generally are treated as institutional clients in all of their financial needs. They are accustomed to bank and brokerage firms who service them through 1–800 numbers and websites, and they generally do not expect a personal relationship with an advisor. Any personal attention is highly appreciated, but there is less resistance to multiple people being involved. At the other extreme, high-net-worth individuals are accustomed to institutionalized service—their CPA firm, their bank, their trust company have all likely surrounded them with teams of people rather than one key contact. That said, many other markets can be addressed by an institutionalized strategy, as long as it is well differentiated.

Many firms have a hard time switching from a personalized business development mode to a more institutionalized mode. After all, usually the firm has been built on the strength of the personal network of the founders, and it is difficult or counterproductive to replicate that institutionally. For example, if the firm has grown through Bob's network and connections, but wants to now become a large investment manager, it will be very inconsistent to continue relying on Bob or sending Bob juniors to every country club in town. It might be better to seek sources of new business that lend themselves to an institutional approach. Examples of such sources include CPA firms, banks, direct marketing to consumers, broker-dealers, or other networks of advisors, custodial or broker-dealer platforms, and so on. Identifying such opportunities is not easy or inexpensive, but relying on personal networks promotes the rent-the-owner model even if we increase the number of people involved.

4. **Behave like a large firm.** The first step to becoming a large firm is believing that you are one. This means that your firm will have to transform its culture from relying on personal relationships and opportunistic communications to being driven by procedure and structure. This sounds scary to most advisors and they see pending bureaucracy and politics in that transformation. However, nothing is further from the truth—personality and entrepreneurship can exist even in the largest firms, as long as they are directed toward the institutional goal. What has to go, however, is the haphazard approach to service, data gathering and documentation and the "shoot-from-the-hip" decision-making.

   It is very common to see advisory firms using their size as an excuse for operational difficulties or mistakes, poor hiring decisions, or lack of progress on important initiatives. If a firm wants to grow it really has to shed that mentality and aspire to behave and act like the larger image it wants to grow into.

   Essentially this means a shift of focus from relationships to results. Most of the management decisions in smaller firms are driven by relationships—"He is a great guy!" or "He is not very good at that, but he is very loyal." The reality in a larger firm is that there has to be a focus on results—there really is no way to accommodate the larger number of people in a relationship-based management. The statements should turn to "He is great guy, but his performance was below his potential this year," or "He is not good at this, therefore we need to hire somebody else who can do that job." Again, this may sound rather cold and impersonal, but in fact it is the only fair way of treating a larger group of employees, so it is either a results-driven approach or a small firm forever.

5. **Become CEO and executives and establish a decision-making infrastructure.** Many advisors are uncomfortable with the responsibility of acting like CEOs. In particular, they struggle with managing people and accepting responsibility for the decisions made. The stakes, however, only

get higher and the responsibilities get bigger. As a firm grows, the size of budget decisions will increase, the complexity of the operations model will increase, and managing the people in the firm will become more difficult.

The burden can be crushing. You hear advisors saying, "I don't want to be the bad guy," or "I don't want to be between the two of you." Unfortunately, that's what a CEO or an executive does—they make tough decisions under stress and with the potential of upsetting people. As my grandma often said, "You can't make an omelet without breaking some eggs."

The decision-making process and interaction of the partner group has to change as well. Most small firms are driven by a consensus process. As the partner group grows, consensus may become impossible or impractical. It is important that the partners are prepared for the transition and have the resolve to carry it through.

6. **Invest in people and develop a mentality of investing in people.** In any service business, financial advice included, the quality of the professionals involved is a critical factor for the success of the firm. Professionals, however, are rarely widely available in the market and the price of talent is high. This puts an enormous premium on firms that are good at developing people. An advisory firm that does nothing else but creates a reliable process for developing professionals is guaranteed to be successful almost regardless of any other factor discussed here.

It is difficult for the owners of most firms, however, to shift their focus from clients to people. It is a scandalous but probably true statement in most large firms that the development of professionals is more important than client service. I don't mean that you should neglect clients, but if you have a chance to provide a young professional with a training opportunity, even if that "displeases" an important client, the scales should perhaps tip in favor of the employee (by no means suggesting risking any damage to the client's financial interests—just their ego). Unfortunately, too many times firms pull out younger professionals from key assignments at the first sign of trouble.

Budgets should also support hiring, perhaps even ahead of demand, once a firm enters into a stage of trying to institutionalize itself. Recruiting and training is definitely scalable as accounting firms can attest, and that's why they hire entire classes of new employees.

7. **Think in terms of expert jobs and set the foundation for departments.** In smaller firms, tasks are simpler, but diverse, and most positions are hybrids in nature, that is, they can easily be split into multiple jobs. Larger firms tend to bring more complex tasks and specialized processes, requiring that the firm retools itself with specialists rather than diverse

generalists. This is a painful process since the "Swiss army knife" employees are incredibly valuable in the early stages and tend to have a problem specializing later as the firm needs change. The earlier the owners start thinking about specialization and encouraging employees to focus on fewer but deeper skills, the less painful this process will be.

8. **Establish a culture of firm ownership of clients.** Finally, for all of this to hold together, everyone should share the deep fundamental belief that the clients are clients of the firm—not just legally, but in terms of who the relationship is with and what the role of the professionals is in this relationship. This is where wirehouses go wrong very often in their efforts to institutionalize their business model. They follow many of the steps we discuss above, but they create a culture of personal ownership of the client promoted by the compensation process and the branch management priorities. A professional who believes that this is "my" client will actively undermine every other step taken to institutionalize the relationship, whether they do that consciously or not.

There are many successful firms in the industry today that generate great income for their owners and have wonderful staff and clients. The vast majority of them will be dependent on the owners for the length of their career and will then dive into a risky process of trying to reinvent themselves around a new generation of owners or under institutional ownership (or both). There were many coffee shops in Seattle before Starbucks and there are still plenty left. Only a couple of them, however, became a nationwide chain with amazing growth and return to its shareholders. Similarly, there will be only a few firms that cross that bridge between an institutional strategy and a rent-the-owner strategy. For each firm, however, the more of these eight issues it can address, the higher its value will be and the more sustainable its growth and success.

## Notes

1. Kathleen McBride, "2010 Top Wealth Managers Report," AdvisorOne, July 2010.
2. Survey conducted by Fusion Advisor Network in 2011 among visitors to fusionadvisornetwork.com. Results have not been published previously.
3. "Real Deals 2010: Definitive Information on Mergers and Acquisitions for Advisors," produced by FA Insight and published by Pershing Advisor Solutions.

# CHAPTER 10

# Managing Professional Compensation

One of the most drastic and difficult changes that comes with the growth of an ensemble firm is the change in professional compensation. Inevitably, as the firm adds employee advisors, it has to go from individually tailoring compensation to the needs, contribution, and history of each employee to having a compensation system driven by internal philosophy and logic. That compensation system is not easy to create, it is uncomfortable to transition to, and it feels a little suffocating at first. However, a good professional compensation system is the only way in which a firm can offer career path and income progression to multiple professionals.

Individual negotiations start being problematic as soon as the firm has more than two or three employee advisors and become practically impossible in an environment with more than five employee advisors. Some of the partners may also be recent additions to the ownership group and thus be "quasi-employees" themselves. In many firms in fact, the partner compensation process will use the same logic and philosophy of the nonowner compensation. In other words, t, install a sound professional compensation process as soon as you hire your second employee advisor.

The biggest disasters I have seen on the P&L of investment advisory firms have come from poor compensation decisions. In the absence of logic and process, firms can easily talk themselves into offering unsustainable levels of compensation or compensation that has no internal equity. It is not uncommon to see the following:

- Firms where one or more employees are making more money than the owners.
- Firms where employees do not want to be owners because the employee compensation is richer.

- Firms where many employees will quit immediately (and slam the door) if they were to find out their colleagues' compensation.
- Firms where two employees in the same position have compensation that differs by more than 50 percent.
- Firms where the supervisor of an employee is paid less than the employee.
- Firms where the top performing employee is paid less than the worst performer.

The list can go on for a while and is not at all that uncommon. In this hit-list of compensation dysfunction we can start seeing the emerging criteria for a good professional compensation system. Namely:

1. The compensation process has to be logical and the logic has to be understood by employees.
2. The pay has to be affordable to the firm.
3. Compensation has to be consistent with the organizational hierarchy and career path.
4. Being a partner should be financially more attractive than being an employee.
5. There should be a sense of internal equity (sense of fairness).
6. It should probably reward performance.

To ensure that all the criteria above are met, we need to start the design of a compensation system with a well-thought-out compensation philosophy.

## Compensation Philosophy

A compensation philosophy is a statement similar to the strategy or value proposition of a firm. It is a succinct description of how compensation works in a firm and what the principles that govern compensation decisions are. It may be somewhat of an abstract statement, just like the strategy, and in fact it should probably relate to the strategy. At the same time, it should be clear enough that it can be applied in practical situations without ambiguity.

Compensation philosophy should cover the following categories:

1. How does compensation in the firm relate to the general market for that position? Do you seek to pay at the average market salary level or in the top quartile? How do you measure the market level of compensation?

2. What are the factors that drive compensation in your firm? What is the priority order of those factors? There are some common factors that deserve our attention:
   **a.** Tenure and loyalty. Will working more years in the firm lead to higher level of compensation?
   **b.** Degrees and designations. Will getting a CFP designation lead to an increase in pay? Will obtaining a license change the salary of an employee?
   **c.** Responsibilities. Within a position there is always variability in responsibilities, including training other employees, special projects, or elements from another position. How will those be paid?
   **d.** Experience. As employees come into the firm and accumulate experience within the firm, how will experience be compensated?
3. Performance. How is performance measured and how does it impact compensation? Is individual performance more important than the performance of a team or the firm? How are they balanced?
4. Incentive compensation. What is the role of incentive compensation in overall pay.
5. Benefits. What is the role of benefits in the compensation plan?
6. Long-term compensation. Is it possible to earn long-term compensation such as stock options, phantom stock, and other forms of long-term incentives?

This sounds like a lot of items for discussion, so I want to offer Fusion's compensation philosophy as an example for discussion. We communicated to our employees that:

> In Fusion we look to compensate our people at the prevailing market salaries and enhance our employee compensation to the top of the industry through incentive compensation. We routinely consult industry surveys to construct our salary ranges for each position and we target to be around the median of the industry. Within salary ranges, employees advance based on their experience, responsibilities and relevant degrees and designations. We create rich incentive compensation programs that add between 5 percent and 25 percent of the salary to an employee's compensation. The incentive compensation is driven by both individual performance and firm performance. We offer industry standard benefit plan that provides for health care and retirement planning for our people.

Note some of the points implied in the statement:

> In Fusion we look to compensate our people at the prevailing market salaries and enhance our employee compensation to the top of the

industry through incentive compensation [Salaries will take you to the market level; bonuses will take you to the top]. We routinely consult industry surveys to construct our salary ranges for each position and we target to be around the median of the industry [This is how we measure the market]. Within salary ranges [Salaries are a range—not a point but there is a limit to variance], employees advance based on their experience, responsibilities and relevant degrees and designations [Tenure is not a factor, we need to define what are the relevant degrees, a little vague on how we measure experience and responsibility]. We create rich incentive compensation programs that add between 5 percent and 25 percent of the salary to an employee's compensation [Defining a range for incentive compensation is a double-edged sword—it can set more reasonable expectations or encourage unreasonable ones. There is a tendency for employees to assume 25 percent]. The incentive compensation is driven by both individual performance and firm performance [You may do exceptionally well in our firm, but if the firm does not do so well you will not get the maximum bonus]. We offer [an] industry standard benefit plan that provides for health care and retirement planning for our people.

## Setting Salaries

Salaries provide the most effective form of compensating employees based on the market value of their job, while at the same time promoting the interests of the employer and the notion of "one firm." Salaries apply very well to all positions in an advisory firm, including the partners and with a few exceptions they are very effective in communicating the statement that each employee works in the best interest of the firm. In contrast, variable compensation (payouts) tends to promote the formation of individual silo books of business. Payouts are more difficult to benchmark and inevitably encourage the perception of each professional as an independent economic agent. My father who owns a shipbuilding business would tell me that in good times every employee wants a percentage of the business and in bad times every employee wants a salary. This "defense of salaries" is necessary since salaries are not the default base compensation for team members in the vast majority of broker-dealer based organizations. The payouts tend to prevail there due to cultural and perhaps regulatory reasons. I would argue that even in those environments, salaries can be a better way of compensating team members who are not principals.

The setting of salary ranges is usually done through the use of salary surveys. Many surveys are available in the advisory industry, including the following:

- The Moss Adams Survey of Compensation—issued every other year and available from www.mossadams.com.
- FA Insight Compensation Survey—issued every other year and available from www.FAInsight.com.
- FPA Compensation Survey—available at www.fpanet.org.

There are also a number of generic (non-industry-specific) surveys that can be helpful in cross-referencing positions that are not very industry specific. Those include many of the general administrative positions.

Usually the salary range of a firm is set with the industry average as the midpoint of the range. For example, if the survey shows an average salary of $50,000, the range can be set to be between $40,000 and $60,000. This represents 20 percent variance on both sides of the average. The 20 percent band is a very typical decision. Of course, not every firm will choose to pay the average compensation. If your compensation philosophy is to pay at the top of the market, then you will need to look at the top quartile in the survey or even the top 10 percent (many surveys may not report this number). Similarly, if your compensation philosophy is to pay at the lower end of the market, you can look to the lowest quartile in the surveys as the center of your range.

When you use a salary survey to set compensation ranges, you should ask the following questions:

- Are the job descriptions in your firm similar to the job descriptions in the firms in the study? In other words, are you comparing apples to apples? Most surveys will contain at least a basic job description for the positions surveyed.
- How many firms participated in the survey and is this number enough to make the survey representative and valid?
- Is there any bias in the survey data that should be accounted for? For example, does the survey attract primarily RIA firms or does the firm attract primarily large firms?
- Do the results of this survey vary substantially from other similar surveys? Can you explain the variance?

The movement within the range should be driven by the compensation philosophy, and this is where you can incorporate factors such as the following:

- Experience.
- Degrees and designations.
- Increase in responsibilities within the job description.
- Tenure—may or may not be a desirable factor.

## Payout-Based Compensation

I just spent an entire paragraph criticizing the payout compensation methods, but I would also acknowledge that many firms use such compensation due to broker-dealer requirements (sometimes regulatory, sometimes purely managerial in nature). If you use payout compensation for professionals, the first important step is to still create an employment agreement that the professional works for the firm and not for herself or himself. In a wirehouse environment that can mean creating a "letter of understanding" type of document that states that the individual should focus on advancing the interests of the firm and not his or her own book of business.

In setting payouts for employees (not for producers renting space from your firm) you can turn to compensation surveys for wirehouse/broker-dealer firms. The magazine *On Wall Street* (www.onwallstreet.com) publishes an annual survey of compensation that fully discloses the grids of all the major broker-dealers.

The payouts from the survey should be a point of departure for your analysis rather than a direct decision point. The payouts in those surveys should be adjusted for the following:

- Who is responsible for generating the leads and the clients the professionals work with? The assumption in wirehouse surveys is that the professionals are generating their own leads.
- How can you adjust the grids to reflect the actual revenue responsibility of the professional?
- How can you incorporate the other factors for compensation such as designations and experience?
- Are you going to create a grid for each level of revenue or are you more likely to focus on one specific number?

Overall, I would still advise most firms to look for ways to create a salary-based plan for compensating their professionals. Still, if the payout system is a must, then you should still go through the exercise of defining your compensation philosophy and seeking ways to implement it using the payout.

## Incentive Compensation

Incentive compensation plans should always be heavily customized and tailored to the individual needs of each firm. Using a "template" incentive plan is a sure recipe for disaster, much like borrowing somebody else's clothes—in the best-case scenario it will be embarrassing. A good incentive plan should support the strategy of the firm, be affordable to the firm in its cost, encourage the right behavior, minimize unintended consequences, and create a strong tie to individual and group performance. It will be very difficult to meet all of the above criteria while adopting the plan of another firm.

There are a number of questions that you should ask yourselves as owners when designing the plan:

- What should be the potential of the plan and its role in the overall compensation of employees? What percentage of the total compensation should come from the plan?
- Should the plan always pay, regardless of the financial results of the firm, or should there be scenarios when the plan generates no income to the employees?
- What are the factors that should influence the plan? How will those be measured?
- What is the balance between individual performance and team performance? What should happen to a great performer in a poor team? What about a poor performer in a great team?
- How will the plan be funded—what will be the funding mechanisms (percentage of revenue, percentage of profit, etc.)?
- How will the plan be administered? Is it going to be transparent? Who will administer the plan?
- How often will the plan pay and what will be the tax consequences to employees and the firm?

Without oversimplifying the topic, the answers to these questions should provide a good idea for the direction that the plan can take. There is a large number of possible plans available to meet the objectives of a firm. Still, the examples below may serve as a starting point for the plan you adopt. They are not meant to be templates but rather "straw men" in which you can poke holes in order to design yours. They are also not meant to be an example of compliance with your FINRA and/or SEC policies and procedures, and your individual plan should be reviewed by your compliance officer.

## Bonus as Percentage of Salary Based on Performance Evaluation

Simple plans are often the most effective, and the intention of this plan is to be simple and to tie the bonus to the performance evaluation of an employee. Naturally, in order to implement such a plan you will need to have a well- functioning performance-evaluation process. To implement this plan simply:

- Define a range of possible bonuses as a percentage of the salary of the employee—for example, between 5 percent and 20 percent of base salary.
- Define the performance evaluation score that will drive the plan—for example, the overall evaluation score. Alternatively, it could be tied to each category of the performance evaluation.
- Assign a value to each level of performance.

For example, let's say that bonuses can be between 5 percent and 20 percent and the bonus will be based on overall performance:

- If the employee achieves a score of 4.5 or higher on a 5.0 scale—that is, excellent performance—he or she will earn the maximum bonus of 20 percent of their salary (e.g., 20 percent of $50,000 = $10,000).
- If he or she achieves a score of 4.0 to 4.5 on a 5.0 scale—that is, very good—he or she will earn a 12.5 percent bonus (e.g., 12.5 percent × $50,000 = $6,250).
- If the score is 3.5 to 4.0—that is, good—he or she will earn a 5 percent bonus—(e.g., 5 percent × $50,000 = $2,500).

Instead of the overall evaluation, you can also tie the bonus to specific categories. For example, you can designate each category as being worth 4 percent if the maximum score is achieved, 3 percent for very good performance, and 2 percent for good performance. Then you can rate the employee on five categories such as client service, recognizing opportunities, supporting the lead advisor, growing expertise, and execution of firm projects.

This simple plan works well if you have confidence in your salary determination (employees see them as fair) and performance evaluation (seen as fair). It is simple to administer, ties to performance, and if the performance evaluation is tied to the strategy of the firm, then it will encourage the right behavior. The drawback is that it is very individualistic —there is no team component. It will also not work well if there are concerns over the performance evaluation process.

## Team-Based Bonus Pool

Unlike plans that are tied to individual performance and therefore individual salaries, team-based plans usually set up a pool of money to be paid out in bonuses. For example, you can set up a pool for bonuses that is tied to the revenue of the business—for example, 5 percent. Let's say the company had $1,000,000 in revenue. This will create $50,000 in the bonus pool. For guidance in setting up the percentage you can look at salaries as a percentage of revenue and then think of what percentage of the compensation should come from bonuses. For example, if salaries are 15 percent of revenue and you want bonuses to be up to 25 percent of the total compensation, then the pool should be around 5 percent of the revenue. Mathematically 5 percent in bonuses/(15 percent salaries + 5 percent bonuses = 20 percent total compensation) = 25 percent.

The bonus pool can be contingent on achieving a certain goal. It can also grow faster past the achievement of a certain goal. For example, the bonus pool can be 0 percent if revenue is under $1 million, 5 percent if the revenue is between $1 million and $1.4 million, and 7 percent if revenue is over $1.4 million. This creates insurance that if revenue declines or is not up to expectations, there will be no bonus expense. In fact, many firms got caught in 2008 in a bonus program without a threshold. The result was that they were paying tens if not hundreds of thousands of dollars while their revenue was declining by 30 percent.

The pool of money (say, $50,000) can be allocated based on the following:

- Equal shares—ignores positions and performance.
- Proportionate to salaries—great method if salaries are considered fair. Note that you don't have to disclose the salaries to administer the pool.
- Proportionate to salaries modified by performance—great method in the presence of a good performance evaluation system. May leave some portion of the pool undistributed.

For example, if an employee has a salary of $50,000 out of a total payroll of $200,000 (25 percent), then the employee will receive 25 percent of the $50,000 pool = $12,500. Let's say we modify the bonus based on performance and the employee scored 80 percent of the maximum score. Then he or she will receive 80 percent of the maximum or 80 percent × $12,250 = $10,000. This means that $2,500 will be forfeited and may be allocated to other uses or distributed to other employees who achieved a higher score. This, of course, lights up a competitive spark in everybody.

## Multi-Criteria Advisor Plan

In the previous two examples we used first the salary of the employee as a funding mechanism and then we used the firm revenue. In this example we will try to use the revenue managed by the employee as a driver for the individual bonus. This has the obvious advantage of focusing advisors on the revenue they have under their control. The disadvantage may be that this encourages "grabbing and keeping" clients. Let's say that the maximum bonus that can be earned is 10 percent of the revenue managed by the advisors. Let's say Stuart manages $250,000 in revenue and therefore his maximum bonus is $25,000 (10 percent × $250,000 = $25,000).

That maximum bonus can be broken down into four categories:

- Asset retention with a target of 95 percent.
- Organic growth from existing clients of 5 percent.
- Referrals generated from existing clients—minimum of 5.
- Client feedback and satisfaction as measured by the partners.

Each category can be scored on a percentage of the goal or be an "all or nothing" category. In combination the scores will create an outcome between $0 and $25,000. For example, an excellent score in AUM retention, organic growth, and client retention but a poor score on referrals generated will result in a bonus of 75 percent of the maximum (3 out of 4) or 75 percent × $25,000 = $18,750.

This kind of plan works well in firms where client responsibilities are readily identifiable. It does, however, encourage some silo mentality and hoarding of clients. It also does not account for the performance of the firm.

## Business Development Incentive Plan

Business development incentive plans are a topic that is a minefield of its own. Many firms believe that if they only had the right incentive plan, they would somehow magically start a flow of new business from their employees. I am personally very skeptical that the incentive plan is the problem why employees do not generate new business. That said, a good sales incentive plan can certainly help motivate those employees that have the skills and the position to develop new clients.

Fee-based firms often use a 15/5/5 plan—15 percent of the first-year revenue, 5 percent of the second, and 5 percent of the third year's. The upfront incentive is powerful considering that an advisor can develop $100,000 and more in revenue in a single year. The 5 percent trails encourage retention of the client and create a bit of a sense of "cultivating" income rather than just turning business development into "hunting," to use our earlier parallel. The reason not to continue the 5 percent for the life of the relationship is that it may create too large of a "trail" of income that will become the dominant compensation method for that employee.

Such a plan may require proper licensing of the employee receiving the incentive and may not work well with unlicensed administrative employees.

## Benefits

As a consultant I see benefits as an important part of a comprehensive and well-rounded compensation package. As a business owner, I see benefits as a high expense that is underappreciated if at all appreciated by employees. I have noticed that in negotiations with new employees, the value of their benefits package is always included in their response to the question, "What is your current compensation?" However, current employees when discussing their current compensation always exclude any of the benefits or even bonuses and always focus on the cash compensation, namely, salary. This, of course, is just me complaining and this book is not about my complaints, so I will leave it at that.

Benefits can be a valuable part of the compensation package of an employee, yet they can be surprisingly difficult to provide for a relatively small employer. Companies with less than 20 to 30 employees seem to fall under the radar screen of most benefits providers and are left with only a few and very expensive options.

The best advice I can provide in the area of benefits is to (1) assign the role of a human resource coordinator to the operations manager or one of the partners, and (2) work with a well-qualified and experienced independent benefits firm that can help you with the area of benefits administration. The reason why benefits are frequently underappreciated by employees is because the staff do not understand their benefits package and how best to use it. They are frequently confused by the different health plans offered and the features of each plan. In addition, the firm and the benefits consultants often send enrollment information that is unclear, confusing, and even contradictory. This is not a criticism of the firms but rather the state of health care insurance overall. It is extremely confusing, highly regulated, and frequently changing, thus frustrating equally the employers and the employees. This is where a good benefits firm is worth every penny—they can guide you through the changes necessary and help you achieve your objective.

Retirement benefits are unfortunately another area of confusion and under-appreciation. Tragically, the majority of employees in the firms I have had a chance to observe do not participate adequately in their firm's 401(k) or other retirement plan. This is very discouraging for the employers, especially since those are essentially providing retirement planning for a living. That said many of the larger firms provide safe-harbor profit sharing plans. Smaller firms usually do not offer retirement benefits.

Regardless of what benefits packages you offer, you should offer those consistently to all employees. This is important not only for compliance with nondiscrimination laws but also in order to enforce and promote the consistency of the compensation philosophy of your firm. Doing individual deals with every employee undermines your ability to promote consistency. In particular, I have often seen firms increase salaries because the employee will not use the benefit plan. This is a slippery slope and damages both consistency as well as the salary logic in the firm. The more consistent you are in every area of compensation, the more likely it is that employees will understand and value what you provide.

## Compensation Management Process

Finally, compensation is never static, and there should be a process in the firm for the review of all employee compensation decisions. Employees should understand the process and its frequency and have comfort in the process. Most firms will review salary decisions once a year—usually at the end of the year. It is a good idea to obtain the information from the performance reviews before making the salary decisions. In this way, performance can be incorporated in making salary changes. As you are making the changes to a position, you should evaluate the following:

- What is our philosophy and what factors did we say influenced compensation?

- How have those factors changed—for example, degrees, designations, experience?
- Is the change material and significant—for example, does one more year of experience really matter?
- Is this employee a candidate for a promotion, not just a raise?
- Where are they in the compensation range and how do they compare to other employees in this position?

I have not discussed performance evaluations in any detail, but those are also vital in making compensation decisions, in particular bonus decisions. The frequency of the performance evaluations is a good guidance for the frequency of bonus payments. If you conduct evaluations once a year, then probably the best idea is to pay bonuses one a year. Similarly, if you conduct evaluations twice a year, this gives you the opportunity to pay bonuses twice a year too.

Compensation is a critical decision for the success of your firm. Hopefully you will remember from this chapter that compensation is not a series of individual negotiations with each employee but rather is the result of the application of a common compensation philosophy to individual cases.

# CHAPTER 11

# The Bottom Line

During a summer job in college I had a lady as my boss who ran a temp agency for restaurant staff—servers, bartenders, cooks, etc. Most jobs were daily and the commission paid in cash so she kept an envelope in the top drawer of her desk. There she put all the cash she received from customers in the course of the day. At times she would pull out a note and send one of the employees out for office supplies or other purchases. Some days, usually at noon, she would take out a bunch of notes and go grocery shopping for her household—the office was adjoining her house. Every evening, when we closed the office at 7:00 P.M., she would pull the envelope out of the drawer and count the remaining cash while still talking to her six or seven college kid employees who were getting ready to leave. Some days there would be a lot of cash left and she would reflect on how the business was doing well and how pleased she was with her strategy. On those days she even sometimes handed out small cash bonuses. Some days there would be very little left and she would go into a long speech about how we needed to work harder and how we needed to find new sources of revenue. Then there were days when what was in the envelope was not enough and she had to open her own purse—you wouldn't want to be there on those days.

That little business in far-away Bulgaria may sound very primitive in its ways but believe it or not, this is exactly how many (if not most) small business owners think of managing their finances. The only difference is that the envelope is replaced by a bank account and the purse with a credit line. Money goes into the banking account, money comes out, and the balance tells you if you are doing well or not. When the personal bills arrive—hopefully there is enough in the account to meet those needs. When there isn't enough money to pay a bill or cover payroll, then the credit line provides the backup needed. There might be available QuickBooks or other financials software and perhaps a spreadsheet or two, but at the end the owner looks at the bank account to tell if the business is doing well.

Service businesses (financial advice included) can appear deceptively simple to manage from a profitability standpoint since the price does not fluctuate much and you don't have to make daily purchasing or inventory decisions. Essentially you hire a bunch of people, pay them to work for you, and make sure you have more revenue than payroll—right? I guess you have to rent an office and buy them computers but by and large, if you can manage the payroll to revenue ratio well, you will do fine, right? This simplistic notion of managing the financials of an advisory firm unfortunately often leads to a distorted picture of the profitability of the firm, and it is surprising how many firms in the industry operate at suboptimal levels of profitability and even at a loss.

## The Owners' Personal Income and Income Bogey

If we say that many firms have "suboptimal profitability" (very fancy way of saying "not making as much money as they could and should"), then we should start by defining what is optimal—how much money is enough? To answer this question, we first need to make one very important decision— how to account for owners' compensation. In almost any ensemble firm, the owners' compensation will be almost as large as the rest of the payroll combined and therefore a huge part of the expenses. Yet we will also find that in most firms the owners' compensation is set in a rather arbitrary way, making it difficult to analyze profitability. So how do we begin our analysis?

The simplest measure of profitability in a firm is to look at earnings before owner compensation (EBOC). EBOC is simply the revenue of the firm less the expenses of the firm BEFORE any economic benefit to the owners of the firm—that is, the owners' draws, salaries, bonuses, benefits, perks, and so on. Depending on the size of the firm, this number should range from 45 percent for the super-ensembles to as much as 70 percent for some of the small ensemble firms. For most firms with revenue between $1 million and $5 million the number should be between 50 percent and 60 percent. If the EBOC is below this guideline, we are either looking at a firm that has profitability issues (e.g., overstaffed, high overhead, poor pricing, etc.) or a firm that is extraordinarily well leveraged—for example, one owner surrounded by many productive employees and rather high levels of revenue.

Benchmarking EBOC against industry surveys such as the Moss Adams Survey of Financial Performance[1] or the FA Insight Survey of Financial

Performance[2] can help you to detect if you have issues with profitability at some very basic level. The EBOC benchmarks are available in both surveys. EBOC is also the critical number driving the valuations of advisory firms done by firms such as National Financial Partners (NFP), Focus Financial, and others. They frequently express the value they assign to a firm as a multiple of the EBOC number, since this allows them to remove any discretionary compensation decisions made by the owners.

While EBOC is a good number to look at for guidance on profitability, it turns out that the most important financial statistic about an advisory firm is something I will call the "bogey." The bogey is essentially the total personal income the owner or owners need in order to meet their household expenses and fund the lifestyle they desire. As primitive as this analysis may seem, this bogey turns out to be a very decisive factor in how the practice will function. If the bogey is lower than the EBOC, this means that the advisor can choose to (and is very likely to) invest the remaining discretionary income in the business. It also likely means that the advisor will be optimistic about the future of the business. If the EBOC is lower than the business, then the advisor will have a hard time investing in the firm and will likely see the future as cloudy with a chance of rain.

For example, Jonathan calculates that he needs $20,000 per month to pay for all of his personal household expenses, meaning that he needs an after-tax income of $360,000. Assuming Jonathan has an effective tax rate of 30 percent (just an assumption) he will need a pre-tax income of approximately $554,000 ($360,000 divided by 65 percent). If Jonathan's firm is generating $600,000 in income to him, this means that Jonathan can "cover his bogey" and have approximately $46,000 to invest. On the other hand, if the firm is generating $400,000 in income, then Jonathan will be short of his bogey and will probably be reluctant to invest. Note that Jonathan's life-style is a bit on the expensive side and perhaps there is some analysis to be done on his personal finances.

The bogey is an individual number and has no basis in any research. It is not taught in any finance class that I am aware of, but it tends to play a critical role. Advisors who maintain high personal bogeys—that is, have expensive lifestyles or support many people in their family—tend to feel a very high level of pressure to produce more revenue and also a strong drive to minimize expenses. As a result, they tend to create firms with bare-bones staffing and high dependence on the owner. They are also frequently willing to seek high-revenue opportunities at the expense of recurring revenue (e.g., life insurance). The opposite is also true—advisors who have relatively low bogeys tend to be willing to invest in staffing, take risks with people, and be much more patient in developing recurring revenue and revenue sources that require time to come to fruition. As a result, firms whose owners have lower-cost lifestyles tend to be more sustainable and with a much higher ability to withstand the pressures of a down market than firms that need to pump out income to the owners.

If you want to calculate your own bogey, you can do so through a very basic personal budgeting exercise. Just combine all of your household expenses, including mortgages, car payments, phones, and so on. Don't forget to include any debt payments (if any), and set the payments to an amount that will pay the debt down, rather than promulgate it. Add any college expenses present or future as well as any expenses for caring for parents or other family members. In other words, sum up everything you pay for and be realistic about the expenses. Finally, look at the cost of funding retirement as well as any other programs to build liquid assets outside the business. The resulting number is your bogey. To the extent that the vast majority of your expenses are not tax deductible, the after-tax number should be increased to create a pretax level of income needed. The result may be surprising, but this is how much you need the business to generate before you have enough income available to invest into the business.

If the EBOC of your firm is lower than your bogey, then you will essentially be choosing between paying a household bill or a business bill. Which one you chose is a personal choice, but you should be realistic about the situation—either your household or your business (or both) will need to quickly change, otherwise one (or usually both) are in trouble.

---

### SIMPLE VIEW OF PROFITABILITY

Revenue − Firm Expenses

= EBOC − Personal "bogey"

= Income available to reinvest in the business

---

Such a simple concept, but so many times I see advisors who believe they have a very profitable practice but actually are running high levels of personal debt because, as profitable as the practice is, it cannot sustain their lifestyle. You would think financial planners would know better, but as they say— "the cobbler's kids usually run around barefoot."

EBOC, however, is not the best measure of profitability since it ignores the cost of the most important resource in the practice—the owner's labor.

To arrive at a better measure of profitability we need to assign owners a salary number. Such a salary can seem arbitrary—after all, owners can assign themselves any number they want. Still, we need to capture the fact that owners are employees too and price that labor. To cut a long story short, I usually tell clients to "vote" themselves (the owners) a salary between $200,000 and $300,000. The logic is that owners represent a higher level of experience and contribution to the business than employee advisors (since only the most accomplished and best contributing advisors become owners), and employee advisors tend to have salaries between $120,000 and $180,000, based on surveys such as Moss Adams' compensation survey.[3] I admit that this is not the most scientific analysis, but it allows us to construct a full income statement.

## The Income Statement

The income statement or profit and loss (P&L) of an advisory firm should consist of three sections—revenue, direct expense, and overhead. The revenue category is obvious—it will include all revenues from the firm from all sources. If the revenue is "haircut" by a broker-dealer, then that haircut will be an offset to revenue (rather than expense), and the income statement will report a net revenue number.

The direct expense in an advisory firm is the equivalent of the cost of goods sold for a retailer or a manufacturer, except the cost is in the form of people rather than materials or inventory purchased. The direct expense is the category reserved for compensation to the professionals of a firm, that is, the staff delivering services to client. Professionals are all staff that carry titles such as advisor, associate advisor, service advisor, analyst, portfolio manager, financial planner, and so forth. It will NOT include staff with titles such as client service administrator, administrative assistant, and so forth. Those will be part of the overhead. The direct expense should also include all the incentive compensation as well as the benefits to professional staff. In practice, many firms report their benefits as one line in overhead, rather than split benefits to professionals and benefits to other staff, and that is usually not a very significant distortion to the income statement picture.

Overhead will capture all other operating expenses: administrative staff salaries and benefits, rent, technology, office expenses, and others. Here firms also include their marketing expenses, their travel, staff development, and other items. All items should be reflected at fair market price and should be directly related to the business. For example, if you own the building you reside in, you will reflect rent at the going market rate for this class of space. In addition, if you pay personal and household expenses through the business (don't—just don't do it!), this should not be part of the P&L of the business. For example, you pay your family's cell phones from the business; those should not be part of the P&L, but yours should.

At this point I can never resist a lecture on mixing personal and business expenses. I can't resist it because I see it every day and I also see the damage it can do. Charging personal expenses through the business will do the following:

- Potentially get you in trouble with the tax authorities.
- Distort the real profitability of the business.
- Encourage you to spend too much ("It's through the business").
- Create the wrong atmosphere in the office as employees will know and notice.
- Drive your partner(s) crazy and encourage them to do the same and spend as much as you do.

The benefit of this frequent practice of mixing up personal and business finances is minimal (and likely in violation of the tax code) while the damage is substantial. There is my lecture—I know you will ignore it, but just as your doctor will tell you to quit smoking every time she sees you, I feel the need to nag again and tell you to quit billing personal expenses through your practice.

Any unusual expenses or expenses considered to be "one-time" in nature can be reported below the operating profit line as "income or loss from nonoperating activity." For example, if there is earned interest on the business cash account, you can report that here.

Presenting the income statement as a percentage of revenue is known as "common-sizing" the income statement and is a great technique for comparing firms of different sizes but with similar economics. It also is very revealing of the dynamics between the difference sections of the income statement. This common-sized income statement is available in practically all the industry financial performance surveys and should serve as your first line of benchmark analysis.

Mark Tibergien, one of the best known consultants and executives in the industry and my mentor in this business, pioneered the guideline shown in Table 11.1 for financial advisory firms, and this guideline has held true for the last 10 years, even with the many fluctuations in the market and the continued increase in compensation cost.

**TABLE 11.1**  Guideline for Common-Sized Income Statement

| Category | Suggested Percent of Revenue | Description |
| --- | --- | --- |
| Revenue | 100 | All net revenues of the firm |
| Direct Expense | 40 | Professional compensation |
| Gross Profit | 60 | Measure of the profitability of services delivered |
| Overhead | 35 | Administrative staff, rent, technology, etc. |
| Operating Profit | 25 | Profitability of the firm |

The normal operating profit of a firm should be 25 percent when all expenses, including owner compensation, have been accounted for. Note that if, for example, the firm has two owners who are the only professionals in the firm, the total EBOC (earnings before owner compensation) will be 65 percent (40 percent professional compensation to the owners and 25 percent profit). This is why it is important to pay the owners a salary—otherwise we cannot arrive at a true picture of the profitability of the firm.

Not every firm will have this neat common-sized income statement, and there are many reasons outside of poor management why those ratios will fluctuate. Here are some of the most common:

- The firm has invested in one or more new professionals resulting in a higher than benchmark direct expense.
- The firm has a highly systematized service process that uses more administrative rather than professional staff—this will result in low direct expense but high overhead.
- The firm has secondary lines of business such as benefits and retirement benefits (higher overhead—lower direct expense) or insurance (higher direct expense).
- The firm is growing rapidly—this will likely result in high expenses overall as the owners are "remodeling" operations and client service.
- The firm is in a high-cost urban center (reserved for Manhattan, downtown Chicago, and perhaps downtown San Francisco)—this will likely result in very high rent and also high compensation cost.

Reviewing the common-sized income statement quarterly or at least every six months should be a habit of all owners. When differences from the past and from the benchmarks occur, they should be seen as reasons to examine and understand better what is causing the difference and how the firm can correct it (if negative) or take advantage of it (if positive).

## Managing Engagement Economics

The most difficult aspect of managing an advisory firm from a financial perspective is managing the engagement-level economics. Unlike manufacturing or retail where every unit produced is largely produced at the same price and will sell at the same price (within some period of time), in the advisory business every client is different. They all likely pay a different dollar amount for the services they receive since they all have different levels of assets under management, and they don't receive the exact same service, either.

Consider two clients. Client A has a little less than $2 million under management and wants to meet with the advisor every quarter to discuss the progress of the portfolio and his plans. He prefers to meet in his home in the suburbs of Chicago and usually on Saturdays since he is a busy corporate executive. He also frequently calls the office with questions and often needs cash out of his account to fund various side activities and businesses. Client B has $500,000 in assets under management and is happy with once-a-year meetings in the advisor's office. He very rarely calls and he continues to add money to his account.

While conceptually both of these clients have signed up for the same service, for example, investment advice, the service they are receiving is not nearly the same. The price they are paying is also far from identical. In fact, it might be difficult to tell who the more desirable client is. On one hand, Client A likely pays as much as 75 basis points on $2 million in assets, equal to $15,000 in fees, while Client B likely pays as much as 110 basis points on $500,000, equal to $5,500 in fees. Clearly Client A is the better client from a revenue perspective. On the other hand, it is also clear that Client A is a "high-maintenance" client while Client B is very easy to work with, but how do we price maintenance? After all, A is paying almost three times more than B! Isn't that enough to pay for some maintenance?

This example is likely familiar to all advisors as all firms have many As and Bs. What this example suggests is that in order to manage the firms to profitability, the advisors have to focus on the following:

- Engagement pricing—How much do clients pay for their services? Clearly just constructing some AUM schedule is not enough.
- Time commitment—Clearly the time of the professionals in the firm is the most expensive and valuable resource, and the use of that resource should be carefully monitored.

- The use of administrative resources—All the calls and the requests for cash and other servicing are handled by the administrative side of the business, and while they don't perhaps occupy the attention of the professionals, they certainly can increase the cost to the firm.
- Complication factor—There is also a "hassle factor" in working with clients. Someone who is requesting Saturday-only meetings at his house will be more difficult to service even if the cost is not necessarily "out of pocket."

## Unit Economics

You can think of the economics of a firm as a collection of the economics of each and every relationship combined into one. In such a sense, each client can be thought of as creating its own small P&L. The P&L might look something like this:

Assets under Management (AUM) × AUM fee

+ Other revenue from the client (e.g. planning fees)

= Revenue from the client

Less: Cost of professional time spent in meetings and other interaction with the client

Less: Cost of professional time dedicated to managing the client's accounts and plans

Less: Any trading cost, research cost, platform fees, and so on absorbed by the firm

= Gross profit from the client relationship

Less: Overhead attributable to the client (e.g., mailing cost, travel, meals, etc.)

Less: Cost of support staff time dedicated to working with the client

Less: Other cost

= Profitability of the relationship

Clearly, doing such an analysis for each and every client will be an "overkill" of the concept and will only appeal to someone with a degree and a passion for cost accounting. Still, if we keep this P&L as a framework, we can arrive at a more practical way of measuring the profitability of a relationship.

It is immediately apparent after a single glance at the client P&L that the major cost of the relationship is going to be in the form of professional time, so we will need to price the cost of time for professionals and perhaps other staff in the firm. The simplest way of doing that is to take a professional's total cost to the firm (salary, bonuses, benefits, taxes, etc.) and to divide that amount by the time available to work with clients (not all the time spent working).

For example, if a professional is paid $120,000 in salary, $30,000 in bonuses, $15,000 in benefits, and costs the firm $35,000 in payroll tax and other costs, then the total cost to the firm is $200,000. Let's assume that the professional has 1,000 hours available to work with clients (most professionals will spend between 1,000 and 1,600 hours with clients—where the rest of the time goes is the subject of a whole other book). Then the cost of an hour of this person's time is $200,0000/1,000 = $200. I am clearly rounding a lot to make my math easier, but having at least a rough notion of the time cost of professionals will help you a lot with thinking about client profitability. Just do this simple math.

So now assume that Client A (the difficult one) was consuming a total of 20 hours of an advisor's time, while Client B was taking 5 hours of time. The gross profit from relationship A would be $15,000 in fees against 20 × $200 = $4,000 in cost or $11,000 in gross profit. Client B generates $5,500 in fees against 5 × $200 = $1,000 in cost. Clearly the gross profit from Client A is much higher and well worth the hassle, BUT the gross margin (percentage) on Client A is 73 percent ($11,000/$15,000) while the margin on Client B is 82 percent ($1,000/$5,500). If we can somehow replace Client A with four Client Bs we will be much better off financially. Plus we will have our Saturdays back.

Problems like this cannot be just left to intuition to solve. On a single-case basis we might be able to gauge the economics of the relationship and the trade-offs, but once you accumulate 200 such relationships it becomes nearly impossible to accurately tell where your profitability comes from. The choice between one Client A versus four Client Bs is a choice of strategy. What clients you pursue and what kind of services you chose to provide should be a decision that goes beyond the mechanical calculation of hours and fees. Still, as you are making these choices you need to be able to perform this type of analysis.

Most advisory firms tend to follow a strategy of maximizing revenue rather than maximizing profit. The philosophy is that the marginal effort of servicing the bigger accounts will grow much slower than the marginal growth in fees charged. Firms tend to believe that outside of some difficult relationships ("high-maintenance" clients) this will hold true and that a $2 million account is not twice as tough to service as a $1 million account. That may very well hold most of the time, but when it doesn't the results are quite unpleasant.

## Service as a Product

We keep using the term "service" but we have not even tried to define what we mean by this broad term. In reality, what clients receive from one firm is very often dramatically different from what they receive from a firm next door that may be marketing a very similar-sounding service. Parameters of variance include the following:

- Number of meetings.
- Amount and sophistication of financial planning work done.
- Tax advice and degree of tax sensitivity.
- Number of investments included in the account and their complexity.
- The type of report produced by the firm and the level of customization of the reports.
- Treatment of outside assets—those not managed by the firm.

In other words, in the investment advisory industry there are great differences in what clients receive, but the marketing language of all firms is the same. That's like getting a car from one firm and a tractor from another but both being marketed as "transportation." This kind of ambiguity might appeal to a salesperson, but it should scare the bajeebies out of a managing partner.

To guarantee profitability at the client level and minimize the change for unpleasant surprises, each firm is well advised to "productize" (standardize) its services and make that service definition clear to the client. If the firm understands well what it is supposed to deliver to clients, it is in a much better position to make staffing and compensation decisions, as opposed to hiring professionals without any clarity on how many clients that professional can service and how much revenue to expect. This "productization" may also reveal the inflection points—the sudden changes in the relationship between incremental cost and incremental revenue.

## The Pricing Grid

The inflection points—the level of AUM where the quantitative changes in assets become qualitative—are important for not just cost of service but also pricing decisions. Ideally, the break-points in pricing are carefully set to correspond to levels where the client expectations change. For example, if a firm is working with four different clients' segments based on wealth, then the break-points correspond to those four segments. Let's elaborate. Assume the firm has the following segments:

1. A clients—Clients with AUM over $5 million receive customized portfolios and statements, in-depth planning and meetings with their tax advisor, quarterly meetings, and proactive phone calls during significant market events.
2. B clients—Clients with AUM over $1 million receive model portfolios with some customization driven by their occupation or other concentrated asset positions, two meetings per year, and proactive e-mails during significant market events.
3. C clients—Clients with AUM over $500,000 receive model portfolios, one meeting per year, and e-mail communications.
4. D clients—Clients with AUM under $500,000 receive model portfolios, meeting over the phone, and a newsletter.

In the presence of these service levels, I think it will be difficult to set pricing points that do not correspond to the client segments. The introduction of the new level of services and the new level of attention naturally allows the firm to enter into a different pricing range on the assets.

It is my impression that most firms charge a retroactive grid, which reprices all assets once a certain level is reached. For example, if the client goes from $900,000 in AUM to $1,100,000, then the fee goes from 100 basis points to 90 basis points on all assets. In other words, the fee goes from $9,000 to $9,900. There is nothing wrong with retroactive grids, and they are easy for the client to understand. The only friction occurs near the break-points where the shift from one level to another causes a rather abrupt change in the fees.

As the industry gets more competitive, though, it should be noted that prospective grids, those that charge a different fee for different levels of AUM, create a powerful "optical" effect of fee reduction and allow for deeper fee cuts for the higher levels of AUM. For example, the two grids shown in Table 11.2 produce the exact same fee for a $10 million AUM client, but the prospective grid appears so much more price competitive.

My experience has been that if asked, a client paying the prospective fee schedule will answer that they are paying 30 basis points in fees (completely ignoring the prospective nature of the schedule) versus the client paying the

**TABLE 11.2** Example of Prospective and Retroactive Pricing

|  | Retroactive | Prospective |
| --- | --- | --- |
| Under $1 million | 100 | 100 |
| $1 million to $5 million | 75 | 63 |
| Over $5 million | 50 | 30 |
| Client AUM | $10,000,000 | $10,000,000 |
| Fee | $50,000 | $50,200 |

retroactive grid, who will say that they pay 60. Needless to say, a stranger listening to this will likely go to the prospective-grid firm.

I personally hate this kind of gimmicky pricing and by no means advocate it. Then again, I obviously have some ambivalence on the subject if I bring it up. The optical effect of a deep discount is very powerful, and if you think that most clients are smart enough to see through it, you might be surprised. Consider this: Some broker-dealers actually use prospective grids and their clients (financial advisors) without an exception succumb to this same optical effect. Hey, even our tax rates are set on a prospective grid (in the opposite direction). All I am saying is that it can be a powerful tool.

## The Cost of Customizing

Pricing and customization go hand in hand. In fact, in pretty much every kind of business, from furniture stores to restaurants, if you want a different fabric or a different side dish, you may have to pay extra. In both cases and in many others, there are usually choices of fabrics and sides but once you "go out of bounds" you can do it but you have to pay for it. Not so in most advisory firms. In the majority of advisory firms, clients receive significant customization of service without any impact on the cost they pay. The result is often a laborious service process for the firm, resulting in low productivity and often profitability issues.

Every point of customization creates a certain level of disruption to the process and adds cost to the production. For example, imagine that all clients receive the exact same investment performance report. There are no custom reports and there are no "outside" assets reported (assets that are not under the management of the advisor but are reported on the investment reports). In that case, producing performance reports will be a very straightforward process. The system can run the entire batch of reports, taking a few hours to do so, and then after a review of the reports, those are good to go. Now imagine every report being completely different and customized to the needs of the client. Here, someone will have to manually sit down and identify what report was to be printed for what client and then produce the reports one by one, probably taking days if not weeks to do so. The potential for human error is also very high, and some of the reports may have to be redone.

Customization creates a lot of value for clients, but advisors should always measure the value created against the cost of delivery. At some point, there is more value "destroyed" by the cost than delivered to the client. Finding the inflection point is truly an art and a sign of good knowledge of one's clients. Of course, there are tools such as client surveys or advisory boards that can help advisors gauge where the point is where they start adding more cost than more value. The usual suspects are the following:

- Custom reporting, especially inclusion of outside assets or below-the-line assets that have to be entered manually.
- Custodians adopted by exception and where the advisor does not do business regularly (nothing wrong with using two custodians but something wrong with using 10).
- Custom portfolios that cannot be "model-traded"—especially if the firm does model trading as part of its business model.
- Unique investments (especially private partnerships and other alternatives) that are researched and used only for one or two specific clients.
- Unique planning process.
- Unusual services—for example, "Should I lease or sell a boat?" (unless you do this for all clients).

Notice that all of these are "too costly" in the context of a bundled service where the client pays the same fee regardless of the use of these services. There is nothing wrong with such services if you price them separately. That's why the furniture store charges extra for fabrics that are not in inventory. You can certainly have them—you just have to pay the price, and you will if they are this valuable to you.

## Minimum Client Account Requirements

The minimum size of a relationship that the firm will accept as a client is an important decision, especially for firms that do not segment their services and that provide comprehensive planning and investment packages. The simplest way of thinking of the minimum client requirements is to look at the total cost of running the firm and divide it by the number of clients. The resulting "average cost per client" should be a good guideline for minimum client acceptance. For example, if the total cost of the firm (inclusive of salaries, rent, etc.) is $500,000 and you have 100 clients, the average cost is $500,000/100 = $5,000. If a client is paying less than $5,000, they are not covering the average cost of "production" and therefore in the long term, if you add only such clients, you will go out of business.

I am sure that here you are thinking, "But what if I have existing capacity—surely another client is not going to increase my cost by $5,000?" This kind of analysis is what economists like to do on their weekends, and they call it marginal cost (the cost of adding one more client) versus the average cost. Economists will tell us that in the short term you should "produce" (i.e., add clients) for as long as the marginal revenue (the fees paid by a new client) exceeds the marginal cost (the cost that client adds). In other words, they will encourage us in the short term to add more clients if we have capacity, until the point where we run out of capacity. In the long term, however, they encourage us to seek clients where marginal revenue is higher than the average cost (the $5,000). Otherwise the business will see declining average revenue and that means declining profits. Note that at the point when the average revenue becomes lower than the average cost, the business starts losing money.

This basic economic theory does not apply very well to wealth management firms, however, since client relationships tend to be multiyear and therefore there is no such thing as a short term. Advisors generally expect to work with clients for at least five years, and most relationships last for 10 years or more. With that time horizon in mind, there is no short term—you either have to believe that you will have free capacity for the next 10 years before you accept the client, or you have to commit to firing them when you run out of capacity and have better prospects (rather a heartless thing to do). Unfortunately, too many advisors ignore the long-term implications of the relationship and talk themselves in short-term marginal economics. I want to emphasize this again, if you can "fire" smaller clients then it is okay to take on smaller relationships. However, if you are reluctant to let go of clients, then there is no such thing as a short-term capacity utilization.

If you want to raise the bar higher than average cost, you should incorporate the profit margin expectation into the minimum client criteria. For example, if you expect 25 percent profitability from the business and the average cost is $5,000 per client, then in order to generate that profit you will need $5,000/(1 - 25$ percent$) = \$6,667$. If every client generates this much revenue, you will cover the average cost and also generate the desired profit level.

The presence of client segmentation may make this analysis more complicated. If you have a lower level of service where you work with smaller client relationships at a lower cost to the firm and the client, you can adjust the minimum to be below the average cost, since the new client will have a "below-average resource consumption rate"—a fancy way of saying "they are less work." From a cost accounting standpoint you can probably allocate a portion of the cost to the lower service level as well as identify direct expenses—those directly attributable to a specific client. This, however, may be unnecessary complication. It might be enough to simply analyze if the lower level of client service is, say, 60 percent less costly than the average, and then use the average cost accordingly—60 percent $\times$ \$5,000 = \$3,000.

Having too many small client relationships is one of the chronic and frequent problems of young ensembles. There are many legitimate reasons to work with smaller client relationships, but you should always be very careful when you are making an exception for a "friend of an important client" or "potential to grow when he sells his business" whether or not you are simply rationalizing what you wanted to do in the first place.

## Managing Staffing Cost and Productivity

It tells you something about my frame of mind and background that I think of staffing as a financial management decision. Still, staffing expenses, from payroll to bonuses to training, account for 75 percent of the total expenses in an advisory firm. Therefore, there is no higher priority in the financial management of a firm than making sure that you have the right staff and that the staff are productive.

Finding the optimal staffing for the firm is not a financial decision, it is a combination of the strategy of the firm, its client service process, and the skill set of the owner group. Still, affordability is often a factor in such decisions, and the financial statement can provide many signals that the firm needs more staff or that it may be overstaffed.

I have never been a fan of following "mechanical" financial ratios in making management decisions, but if there is one such ratio that proves to be very useful, it will be the revenue per staff ratio. If you simply take the total revenue of the firm and you divide it by the number of people in the firm (including the owners), the resulting revenue per staff will give you a good idea of the productivity in your firm. If the ratio is under $200,000 per staff, then you have perhaps added too many people too early in the growth of the firm. If the ratio is over $250,000, perhaps it is time to hire another person. There are many good reasons to deviate from this norm, and super-ensembles tend to reach very high levels of productivity (as much as $400,000 per staff) without needing to add staff. Still, this mechanical norm has been a good guideline for staffing.

If you think you need another person in your firm, finding out whom to hire may not always be an obvious decision. Some of the questions to consider are the following:

- Do you need to start creating specialized positions rather than using multifaceted job descriptions? This is particularly true in operations.
- Do you need to add a professional or an operations person?
- Is it beneficial to create some redundancy in the process and have more depth at a position?
- Is there a chance to start somebody on a career path to a more senior position?

In particular, balancing the needs of the operations department with the professional positions in the firm may prove to be a challenge. In general, the ratio of professionals to operations staff tends to be a steady one-to-one in most firms, but this does not give you any guidance on whom to hire next—one more operations person or one more professional? Some of the best solutions to this quandary come from firms where the entry-level professionals start their careers in the back office and provide much needed support to their more senior colleagues. This experience also tends to create more rounded careers and help with management responsibilities when the professionals reach that level.

Productivity is a critical factor for profitability in a firm, but it is not always clear and apparent to the firms how to measure it. Most firms prefer not to overcomplicate their internal accounting and management process, but I would suggest that the following simple measures may be very helpful:

- Number of clients managed as the primary relationship manager ("owner")—these are clients that rely entirely on the professional for advice and service.
- Number of clients managed as the "second chair"—these are clients that work closely with an advisor but still see somebody else as the primary relationship manager.

- Revenue under management—revenue from owner relationships.
- Growth percentage of relationships managed—including market and contributions.
- Organic growth in AUM—new assets from existing clients.
- New AUM—new assets from new clients.

This list may seem overly complicated, but in fact most sophisticated CRMs can help you track such statistics. What is more, each of those numbers easily translates into an incentive plan (bonus) measure that can be used.

## Overhead Management

I have found myself countless times sitting down with an advisor, examining their financial statement, and trying to figure out why overhead is so high. Rent will seem to be okay, perhaps a little high, marketing might be a little high but that's what a firm needs to grow, I guess a little high on the travel but nothing too bad. So where is it? The answer is usually "death by a thousand cuts." Seemingly small overhead items can pile up to become a very substantial drag on the profitability of a firm. The most common "barnacles" on the ship are the following:

- Review all of your programs and subscriptions. Very often advisors are subscribed to coaching or marketing programs costing anywhere from $1,000/year to $15,000/year without actually using the programs. Coaching programs are a fantastic way to improve your business, but if you have stopped going to the meetings and using the program, you should consider cancelling your membership.
- Don't overspend on travel and entertainment. There is a tendency to let such expenses run away, especially since many advisors add their personal meals and travel to this expense.
- Refrain from overinvesting in the office. Since many advisors own their building, many look at the improvements in the office as an investment. That said, spending a lot on the office can really tax the practice. You don't want to have a "starving family living in a palace."
- Review benefits carefully. Benefits play a very important part of compensation packages, but when the cost is more than the satisfaction that the employees derive from them, it may be time to scale them back or to create different packages for different levels of employees.

- Scrutinize technology spending. Technology consultants and IT managers can at times be too focused on the technology aspect of a solution. At times, manual solutions are more effective and efficient. Surprisingly so, sometimes it is cheaper and more effective to have an employee spend 20 hours per week on a task rather than spending $30,000/year on a technology solution. IT managers, though, sometimes undervalue or miss such solutions, and you as the owner and managing partner have to promote that perspective.
- Don't let the cell phone bill run out of control. Especially in smaller practices, it is not unusual to see cell phone bills well into the thousands as a result of adding the entire family and everybody being on unlimited plans with multiple options to the contract.
- Remember that car payments through the business are still payments. Simply, don't buy a car just because the payments would go through the business, and don't buy a car through the business you wouldn't buy personally.

## Key Ratios on Your Dashboard

Sooner or later, every decision you make in your firm will be reflected in your financial statements. Everything you do will increase a cost or lower it, increase productivity or require more people, accelerate revenue growth or slow it down. Very often, you will impact multiple financial measures with a single decision. Profitability in a firm (or lack thereof) does not result from spreadsheet analysis or financial manipulation of the P&L (as proved by Enron) but rather from management decisions. That said, management decisions should be made with a full view of the current and forecasted effect they will have on the financials. In other words, the car does not go faster or slower when you look at the speedometer—that's driven by your foot on the gas pedal—however, before pushing the gas pedal further, you may want to look at the dashboard to see how fast you are going.

The following five ratios, in my mind, belong in every dashboard—especially ensemble firms. They are quite popular in the industry, frequently discussed (Mark Tibergien and Rebecca Pomering cover them in depth in their book *Practice Made Perfect*) and also often benchmarked. I want to go over them with a quick view of their effect on ensemble firms.

1. **Earnings before Partner Compensation**—As we said, this is the simplest measure of profitability and should be calculated monthly. It will tell you if your firm has issues with profitability, but it won't tell you much about why those issues occur.

2. **Revenue per Staff**—This ratio will give you the basic measure of productivity and staffing. As we discussed above, the ratio may tell you when to hire and when you are becoming overstaffed. It should be calculated twice a year and be part of your budgeting process.
3. **Revenue per Professional**—The revenue per professional will suggest when you need to hire new professionals rather than operations and support staff. It can be as high as $700,000 to $800,000 in the largest super-ensembles while it is usually lower for smaller firms, closer to $500,000 per professional. Since the ratio can be so variable, your history should be your first benchmark. It should be calculated twice a year and be part of your budgeting process.
4. **Revenue per Client**—This is a critical measure that will show you the size and scope of the typical relationship. The trends in this ratio will reveal if you are working with a more affluent client base or "downgrading." It can also serve as your guideline for minimum client acceptance criteria as well as for determining what services to provide.
5. **Overhead Percentage**—Simply put, it will tell you if you are spending too much on "stuff." Don't let it run away from you, as we discussed above. This percentage should be monitored monthly.

## Budgeting and Financial Management Discipline

A budget is the foundation for measuring performance—we simply can't answer the question "How are we doing?" before we establish "How did we think we would be doing." While external benchmarks can tell you how you compare to other firms, the ultimate guide to where you are is your plan. Similar to running a marathon, you can't just use the other runners as your guideline for how quickly you should run and how well you are running. There are elite runners who finish marathons in the amazing 2 hours and 15 minutes (I can't even bike that fast)—but they are hardly a benchmark for the average casual runner. Roughly 5 percent of the runners in a race would not even finish it—you do not want to be comparing yourself those either. Finally, in every race you will see many runners who will rush by you at the start only to see them walking in pain 20 miles later—again, not the benchmark you want to follow. The best measure of how fast you need to go is a well-thought-out plan for how fast you want to go. In other words, you need a budget.

A good budget will include the full financial statement in enough detail so that you can identify and discuss the more significant financial decisions.

In other words, you don't have to identify "paper clips" as a budget item, but you should have a budget line for "office supplies" since it likely is a material amount.

A good budgeting process will allow the people who make the spending decisions to examine the plans for the coming year and provide the firm with an estimate for what resources they need. In other words, as a managing partner you can't draft a budget for the operations department and then just drop it on them as the new spending limit. The budget for the operations department should be prepared by the operations department and then discussed in partner meetings until an agreement is reached.

The budget should be categorized in such way that you can answer questions such as "Why are we spending too much on . . . ?" In other words, the budgets prepared have to be identifiable on the income statement. Very often two or more departments (or people) will share responsibility for an income statement, and a result we can't tell later who is responsible for the overspending. The classic example is three partners responsible for marketing and each managing a marketing budget. If the marketing expense is too high, there is no way to isolate the cause without a painful investigation. It will be best if each partner has a subaccount line on the P&L.

Finally, the budget should ideally be entered into the accounting package the firm uses, so that you can generate "budget vs. actual" reports, which will serve as the basis for partners' reviews of the financials. All accounting packages that are in common use allow such entry. Some offer more sophisticated budgeting modules, but even if you don't use those modules and prepare your budget in Excel, you can always enter the finished product in the accounting system.

Financial management should serve both as a diagnostic tool when the results are not as good as the firm expected as well as a leading indicator for where the firm is headed. Incorporating the routine review of your financial measures in the partner meetings at least once a month will result in better management decisions. This may sound like a preachy exaggeration, but I have found in my experience that the best indicator of the profitability and success of a firm is how quickly and easily they can produce their P&L and key financial statistics. Firms that have them easily and readily available ("Let me print them for you") tend to be profitable and successful. Firms that struggle producing them ("I'll have to call my accountant—he hasn't finished the fiscal year yet") tend to have high overhead and general issues with growth and profitability. I told you this was going to be preachy, but it's very true—success is a habit, not a singular effort.

## Notes

1. www.investmentnews.com/article/20110411/INCR/110419993.
2. www.fainsight.com/research.html.
3. "2011 Moss Adams Investment News Adviser Compensation and Staffing Survey" reports a median salary for lead advisors of $125,000 and $192,000.

# CHAPTER 12

# The Devil in the Details

Whenever I start discussing operations inside ensemble firms I can't help but remember a client I consulted with. The firm had five advisors, three of them partners, and was fairly large and successful. In terms of operations and technology, they had three of everything—three administrative assistants, three new account processes, three financial planning systems, three billing schedules, and three custodians. Three of everything, one for each partner, except for performance reporting systems—of that they had four—one partner had two. It is critical in an ensemble to maintain uniform processes across the firm and maintain a client-centric, not advisor-centric operations model.

As a business owner, giving up your habits of how you serve clients and what tools you use can be very difficult and stressful. In fact, my experience has been that when it comes to negotiating with your partners, compensation and equity discussions usually get resolved in a couple of months; in contrast, operational disagreements tend to last for years. Still, without agreement between the partners on the service process that the firm will follow it is difficult to function as a team and the results are poor profitability and subpar client service.

### Agreement on Service Process

Achieving agreement on the service process you use as a firm is essential not only for your operational efficiency but also for your overall ability to function and present yourself as a firm. Without a uniform operational process, it will be very difficult for the different partners to share clients. Every new interaction will present clients with a new service process and perhaps a new outcome. There is nothing more undermining to the credibility of the firm than each partner coming up with a different answer and leaving the client to sort out whose recommendation to follow.

The uniformity of process is also necessary for the firm to be able to train and develop staff. Even if the partners have come to a comfort level with the "diverse" processes, the staff will either have to choose which partner they will work for early in their career and therefore adopt that process or spend a significant amount of time learning multiple processes.

A service process agreement is also a necessary part of a good compliance and risk management. If every professional uses different processes, the firm will have a very hard time explaining the discrepancies and the differences in the recommendations that may be made. It also becomes more difficult for the compliance staff to supervise each advisor since they have to approach the supervision differently and understand the different processes used.

Naturally, a good service process starts with the word *process*—in other words, the first agreement you have to reach as an ensemble firm is that you will follow a predictable and systematic path to delivering your advice to clients. The same two clients with the same circumstances and goals should always receive the same advice, executed in the same manner. Every firm will create its own unique service process, but the definition of that process has to include the following areas at minimum:

- What information do you gather from prospective clients and where is that information stored, maintained and secured?
- How do you propose your services to clients and what proposal and other documents are put in front of each prospective client?
- What pricing analysis is performed and how do the professionals determine the price they will offer to the client?
- What legal documents are signed by the client and what disclosures are made?
- How does the firm create financial plans and what is the scope of the plan created?
- What is the primary financial planning tool the firm uses and what are the cases where a professional may chose to use a different tool or customize a plan?
- What is the investment philosophy of the firm and how is that philosophy implemented?
- Who are the investment managers the firm uses (including internal) and how are they used?
- What are the situations in which professionals will customize a portfolio versus use standardized (model) portfolios?

- What are the performance reports used?
- Who are the points of contact for a client and in what situations?
- How often are meetings scheduled and what is the standard preparation for a meeting?
- How often are portfolios reviewed and what is the review process? How are decisions regarding changes made and implemented?
- Who trades client portfolios and how are the trades made?
- How is the clients financial plan and/or investment strategy updated? How is the clients' data kept up to date?
- How often does the investment committee meet and how are the decisions communicated to the rest of the firm?
- What is the quality control process to ensure that no mistakes are made in client plans, portfolios and documents?

This list is by no means complete in terms of all the steps in a process that need to be standardized, but it covers the more common areas where I have observed issues in arriving at an agreement.

I am not in a position to recommend what process your firm should follow, and I am also very skeptical of any "standard" process that might be offered as a template. The process you follow should be a function of your unique client service, and your unique client service should be a function of your strategy. If every firm in the industry offered the exact same services delivered in the same way, we would be essentially commoditizing our own service. The outcome would be an industry where the only remaining differentiator is price.

## Investment Committee

The investment committee of a firm is not an operational unit but plays a critical role in achieving operational integrity. If a firm can achieve agreement on the investments used and the manner of their use and uniformly implement that approach across all partners and professionals, this will usually lead to overall operational streamlining. The worst culprits in terms of deviations from the process are usually related to the investment services of the firm—the portfolios constructed, the managers used, and the exceptions generated.

For this reason, it is good to empower the investment committee to not only discuss and make decisions on the intellectual side of service but also to act as the watchdog for the integrity of implementing those decisions.

A good investment committee should spend time reviewing existing portfolios and discussing the exceptions uncovered and how to standardize those.

I am always surprised how large firms with well-functioning investment committees tend to have a remarkably narrow range of investments in their portfolios. When I was interviewing three of the larger firms in the country on their investment implementation, I found that on average they used no more than 25 to 30 securities in their portfolios. Most of those "securities" were mutual funds or third-party investment managers. In contrast, when looking at actual data from much smaller firms, I can't help but notice that they use on average between 50 and 100 funds, managers, or other securities.

In turning the investment committee into an operational watchdog, it is imperative to have the chief operating officer of the firm be a member of the committee. This may sound like an unusual step, but the presence of someone who is focused on process and efficiency can change the discussion significantly. Of course, for that to be possible you will need to have a chief operating officer and not many firms do!

## Leadership in Operations

Very few advisors have a background in operations. What is more, even fewer advisors have an interest in operations. I realize this is a gross overgeneralization, but I hope that this is one most firms will agree with. Unfortunately, the result of this trend is that when the partners/owners of a firm gather around the table to make decisions, the area of operations is woefully underrepresented.

Every area of the firm should have its leaders and operations are no different. The leadership in operations will ensure that the firm decisions fully incorporate the operational perspective and that staff receive the guidance and training they need. In addition, having a leader in operations will promote the entire area of service and its status within the firm. What often happens in large ensemble firms is that since none of the employees in operations hold high-level positions (executive committee, partners, etc.), the entire area is seen as a "second-class" career. As a result, talented people in operations either seek a career on the professional side of the business or a career outside of the firm.

Providing operations with leadership is often hampered by the evolution of the staffing in a firm as it grows. Typically in the early stages of the firm, the operations area is led by an office manager. Frequently the office manager is an experienced staff person with long tenure in the firm.

Unfortunately, this also means that the office manager usually has very little experience in managing operations for a large firm and has very little access to "outside knowledge." What is more, the typical office manager usually has limited training in management and perhaps is seen by the staff and the partners as a senior administrative assistant.

These generalizations are not meant to question or discount the value of the office managers in advisory firms but rather to encourage firms to prepare them early for the leadership role they will have to play. This can be achieved by:

- Hiring talented and ambitious people for the position who can grow as the firm grows.
- Providing office managers with leadership and management training.
- Exposing your office managers to other firms in the industry and the industry's best practices.

## Customization and Efficiency

When making technology decisions, it is a natural instinct to seek efficiency and try to lower the cost of service by achieving such efficiency. In most services, however, efficiency is not necessarily a goal in itself since the efficiency and the customer experience tend to collide. For example, the most efficient way for a firm to handle its calls is to create a call center. Unfortunately, that is also one of the best ways of alienating all clients. Similarly, the most efficient process for a hamburger restaurant is not to allow any customization—everybody gets the pickles and everything else. Unfortunately, that would send many clients elsewhere. In other words, efficiency is desirable but cannot be a single-minded goal since it always has to be balanced against customer service.

A service firm will always accept a certain level of inefficiency and cost as long as that creates higher value and experience for the customer. The key in operations, therefore, is not to minimize the cost and the efficiency but rather to find that inflection point where further increases in customization add a lot more cost than they add value to the client.

Small firms tend to customize everything for every client. Larger firms tend to try to streamline every single part of their client delivery. The ideal solution will be somewhere in the middle and will be very specific for each firm. Every client demographic and profile will have its own inflection points for customization. Thus every firm needs to discuss the points of customization on its own. That said, the usual decisions that need to be made are:

1. Custom portfolios. Will the firm use custom portfolios or models? Will portfolios be traded individually or traded as a block?
2. Individual securities. Will different clients have a preference for a specific security or asset class? Will the firm add asset classes or securities to accommodate clients?
3. Custom analysis. Should I buy or lease a boat? Should I buy this business? What about this angel-investment opportunity? Such questions are asked often, and the custom analysis necessary to answer them can be costly and laborious.
4. Custom reporting. Will individually created reporting packages slow down the quarterly report production?

Customization can be a source of significant cost, but it creates competitive advantage. What is more, a firm that can create customized solutions efficiently, will have significant competitive advantage. For example, Dell Computers, by allowing customers to customize their personal computer (PC) with their chosen hardware and by producing the custom PCs efficiently, was able to become the market share leader in personal computers.

## Technology Selection

The keys to choosing the technology systems the firm will use are, first of all, a well-developed and understood process, and second, integration. The process should drive the technology used rather than the other way round. The process should stem from the service decisions of the firm and its strategy. The technology should be just a tool for execution. There are many vendors in the industry with diverse and flexible solutions, so there should not be a problem matching the process with the technology available. This is particularly true for CRM solutions and performance reporting solutions where there very highly customizable packages.

Integration of systems starts with the integration of data. The ability of accurate data to reside in each and every system is critical for the efficiency of the firm. For that to be possible, usually you have to decide on which system you will treat as your "core"—the point of origin. For example, if you decide that your main custodian's workstation is your core system, then you will give preference to CRM systems and performance reporting packages that are supported by your custodian. Vice versa, if you consider your performance reporting and trading system to be the core, then you will only consider CRM systems and planning systems that can integrate with the performance reporting system.

Consistent with the theme of uniformity, you need to arrive at a firm-wide system selection rather than an advisor-centric solution. This applies to all aspects of technology, including software and hardware. Many tech employees have been driven crazy by one of the owners wishing to do everything on an iPad while the firm's technology is not capable of supporting that. There is nothing wrong with the iPad, by the way, as long as that's what the entire firm uses.

Unfortunately, there has been a strong tendency in the advisory industry for custodians and broker-dealers to use technology as the "captive" factor. Both custodians and broker-dealers have poured a lot of investment into developing their technology solutions, but they have also made sure that the solutions work only (or just about only) with their own custody or broker-dealer services.

As a result, advisors face a difficult dilemma. On one hand, they can use a broker-dealer workstation that integrates with a specific CRM and specific financial planning software. Further, if they keep all their assets on the broker-dealer platform, they can receive integration of performance reporting with the above packages as well as ease of use of account services. On the other hand, this means that any assets held outside the "platform" are very difficult to deal with operationally. In addition, the chosen CRM may not be the one that best fits the firm.

A somewhat similar process occurs with custodians—the acquisition of performance reporting and rebalancing and trading systems by custodians makes it difficult for advisors to mix and match their custodian needs with the software they want to use. It is perfectly understandable for a company to only develop software that supports its own business. After all, why would a company invest in software that works with its competitor? However, what is unfortunate is that if advisors want to purchase with their own budget a comprehensive "best of class" suite of software solutions, they may find that to be very difficult to do.

## Quality Control and Risk Management

Quality control and risk management have been largely overlooked as areas of emphasis inside advisory firms. The firms that belong to a broker-dealer network usually let the broker-dealer worry about compliance. The firms who are Registered Investment Advisor (RIA) only tend to practice under the assumption that "we know each other well, we trust each other, and we are not doing anything wrong."

Quality control and risk management are critical for the long-term success of a firm. They go well beyond the bureaucratic process of checking boxes and doing paperwork and instead should focus on the quality of the work delivered to clients and the degree to which the work of different professionals may be exposing clients to risk.

The two areas of quality and risk are closely related. After all, some of the risk comes from the ill-intended actions of one of the professionals in the firm, but a lot of the risk a firm may face has to do with the quality and nature of its recommendations. Even well-meaning and well-intentioned advice can create substantial liability for the firm if it proves to be erroneous or misunderstood.

The larger firms in the industry have come to appreciate the extent of such risk and look to embed quality control into the standard operations process. Some of the best tools available are the following:

- Require a peer review and sign off on every financial plan.
- Rotate advisors in a relationship once a year to give another professional a chance to review the work and discuss the service with the client.
- Randomly review portfolios and their associated documentation.
- Require partner sign-off on proposals or other client documents.
- Implement a partner review of the clients for their fit with the strategy of the firm and their risk.

## Vendor and Strategic Partner Choices

Finally, much of the operations of an advisory firm are driven by its strategic relationships—custodians, broker-dealers, and investment managers. The selection or change of these relationships will have a dramatic impact on the operational efficiency and capabilities of the firm, and it should therefore be performed very carefully. Some of the questions to discuss are the following:

- Is the strategic partner really strategic? Does their strategy fit with the strategy of the firm?
- Will the relationship be exclusive or one of many? What do we gain or lose from exclusivity?

- How much of the firm's business will be concentrated with the vendor? Is concentration going to lead to enhanced pricing and service? How valuable is this status?
- What is the durability of the partner? Are they likely to exit the business, change ownership, or change services in the future?
- What is the level of customization the vendor can offer to your firm? Just as you customize some services for your clients, will they customize some of their services for you?
- What will be the customer reaction to this alliance? Is the vendor/partner well known to the clients, and what is their reputation? If clients start researching the vendor, what will they find?

Philosophically, I hold the view that a firm should never become captive to its strategic partner and should seek to implement its own processes that allow for its business to be independent of the vendor, even if that means sacrificing some operational efficiency. We have already seen many examples of changes in strategy, changes in ownership, and changes in pricing to know that relying on the same vendor to be there for the next 10 years is unrealistic. This is particularly true for relatively smaller, privately held investment managers and broker-dealers where we have seen significant consolidation and changes in service.

Operations management in an ensemble firm can be summarized by the words *process, uniformity*, and *people*. With the added number of professionals, partners, clients, and services the firm has to agree on a process and follow that process closely. The ability to establish that uniformity of process will largely create (or destroy) operational efficiency in the firm. Even the best-laid plans, however, are nothing but fancy charts and diagrams without talented and motivated people. The people in operations should be just as important as those in the professional capacity. Their work will ensure that the professional advice reaches the client in the most efficient and effective manner.

# PART III

# What Happens Next

# CHAPTER 13

# Recipes for Failure

So far we have discussed how to painstakingly build an ensemble firm through years of patience, effort, and expense. In this chapter we will briefly discuss how to destroy an ensemble. Granted, most likely you don't need to read a book on how to lead your ensemble firm to failure—it's real easy. All you have to do is act selfishly, fight with your partners, mismanage your employees, let your emotions and reactions roam free, and change your mind frequently. You don't even have to do all of those—just pick two or three that feel very natural to you.

I think I admitted in several chapters that my qualifications are limited in a certain area. However, in writing this chapter I feel extremely well qualified. I have spent a significant part of the last 10 years arguing with my partners and have accumulated expert-level experience on the subject. Most of those arguments only occurred in my head—a process many of you are familiar with—but that did not make them any less vigorous or protracted. Many of them were real, with the ensuing damage to relationships. Some were necessary but most I regret. If the divorce rate in the United States is close to 50 percent, the divorce rate between partners is much higher. Unfortunately, my experience has been that for every partnership that successfully grows, two split up. The reasons are usually many, and perhaps many of those partners should have never come together in the first place, but usually the drama boils down to gradual erosion of the trust and respect between the two or three partners involved.

If you want your ensemble to succeed, you have to maintain the trust and respect of your employees and your partners. You have to remember that if you they lose their respect for you, you will lose their commitment no matter how much you pay them or how much they have at stake. You have to protect and replenish the respect, which means that you have to set high standards for yourself and your behavior. Many business owners feel that since it is their business they should be free to behave based on their instincts. Unfortunately, that frequently backfires. Think of how you modify your behavior in front of your children—your language changes, your demeanor changes, and your actions change. Same for owning a business—if you want to have a good business, you have to maintain the trust and respect of your employees and your partners. This may sound stressful and unfair, but I guarantee you that partnership breakups are even more stressful, and usually both sides believe them to be grossly unfair.

## How to Fight with Your Partner

Partnership issues take a very painful toll on all professionals involved. They create a lot of stress and emotional burdens, and sometimes they fester for years. There is almost no other issue that can poison your life as much as fighting with your partner (save perhaps marriage). The source of the issues between partners often is one of the following:

- Doing only things you like to do—There is an implicit agreement when entering into a partnership that you will modify your behavior to the goals and culture of the firm. Failing to modify your behavior will certainly aggravate your partner and damage your relationship. For example, declaring that you don't like to manage people is not going to be productive since long term you have to. Similarly, refusing to be inconvenienced will result in suboptimal decisions that will get in the way of the partnership. I once had a client who simply refused to go to the firm office because it was too far from his house. As a result, the firm maintained a smaller office where he worked. Needless to say, this is an unnecessary cost and also creates a bad precedent.
- Being selfish—Sharing goes hand in hand with trust. If two partners trust each other, they can design just about any partnership structure and they will still have little issues in allocating revenues, expenses, and profits. Lose that trust and there is almost no structure that can provide comfort and ensure that everyone is receiving their fair share. This is why selfish behavior and the act of trying to sneak a "quick one" past your partners will be so damaging. As soon as one partner is caught in selfish behavior, the trust evaporates and it becomes very difficult to function.
- Not sharing the right information and decisions—Finding the balance between decisions you need to make together and those you can make on

your own is something you learn through experience. It is very easy to go too far in one direction or another. If you meet with your partners over every small decision, you will soon feel that you are both wasting your time and micromanaging each other. If you pull the trigger on too many decisions without consulting your partners, they will feel that you are not respecting their vote. I had an agreement with my partner once that we would use the "$5,000 rule"—if the impact of a decision is more than $5,000, then we need to talk, otherwise, "act on your own judgment." This is a very mechanical approach but can be the start of a process. Better yet, you can start with a mechanical rule and then develop a sense for what you need to discuss.

- Ignoring the deal-breakers—There are always items that may not be very important to you but may be critical to your partner. You have to recognize when that happens and concede the argument, especially if the outcome does not mean that much to you. For example, let's say that you don't feel that the firm should be working with a particular client because they do not meet the asset criteria, but your partner is extremely passionate about accepting them as a client because they remind him of how he progressed through his career. At some point you have to notice the tone of the argument and ask yourself, "Is this important enough for me to lose my partner over?" This does not mean that you have to be blackmailed into accepting decisions you disagree with—most issues will not have this power to change the relationship. However, when you come across a deal-breaker you have to recognize it and avoid it.
- Not respecting the partner meetings—Partner meetings, just like staff meetings, can seem very time consuming and unnecessary. However, they are critical in ensuring that as partners you are communicating and on the same page. They are a good forum for expressing concerns and exchanging thoughts. Systematically cancelling and postponing them is a sure way to undermine your relationship. Excuses such as "We talk all the time" are just that—excuses. A periodic meeting makes sure that you are focused on the state of the partnership and not distracted.
- Being the good guy—In a firm with multiple partners and shared supervisory responsibilities, it is very important to be consistent in your message to employees. Sometimes one partner can try to play the "good guy" or "the cool uncle" and that can be a very corrosive behavior. If you always leave your partner to be the one delivering tough messages to employees, you are undermining the authority of the entire partner group, and you are also likely making your partner very angry.

Partnerships are fragile and rely on trust. The previous list is hardly exhaustive—the best idea is to apply the golden rule—never do to your partner what you do not want him to do to you.

## Losing Control of Your Own Firm

When I asked one of my clients what was the reason he was seeking help from a consultant, he replied, "Last year I took three months of vacation and it wasn't because I wanted time off—I just could not stand to be in the office." This is not an isolated case at all—in fact, most business owners have some fear of their office. What they fear is spending time on activities they do not enjoy and being judged by their employees. This two-headed monster is scary enough to chase away even the bravest of advisors.

A good friend of mine was telling me how at one point he instructed his staff not to approach him with any problems until 10:00 a.m. He was telling me that otherwise he found himself listening to complaints and problems for the first two hours of the day, and it was impossible to retain a positive attitude for the remainder of the day. Managing your emotional energy and spending the day in a way that helps you retain your enthusiasm is a critical technique.

In order to maintain control of your day you need to set some limits for when you are available and when you need some privacy. I highly recommend using a closed door as your sign to staff that you are busy and you need to focus on what you are doing. Establish some routine for when you are available and when you are not, and you will find that you have the ability to step away when you need to. If you fail to do so, you may find you never have time to focus on your priorities and you are constantly dealing with other people's priorities.

I am not trying to advocate that you lock yourself in your office and become inaccessible. On the contrary, I believe it is very important that you spend quite a bit of time with your employees. However, you need to establish a protocol for when that's productive and when you need some privacy. You can use the closed door or you can even establish "visiting hours" or any other. It all works as long as you consistently enforce it and make it clear that it is important to you.

Running an ensemble firm by definition means that you will let other professionals participate in decision making. In fact, you will likely invite them to help you make decisions and even criticize the decisions you have made in the past. This criticism, if constructive, can help you create a better firm. However, at some point the criticism can become caustic and toxic, and you want to quickly draw the line between what is acceptable criticism and what is going too far.

I have personally experienced firms where a key employee believes that the strategy and direction of the firm is not optimal or just wrong and spends every meeting berating the quality of management and the quality of the firm. Being aware of your deficiencies is important, but if every meeting turns into a session of self-flagellation, then as an owner you will find yourself on the defensive and sooner or later will start dreading the next meeting. When that happens, I am a believer in drawing the line and letting everyone know that you are the boss and that you bear the responsibility for your decisions.

My grandpa told me this story about Christopher Columbus. The story is likely pure fiction but has stayed with me all these years. Columbus will meet frequently with the nobles on his ship and they frequently expressed their discontent over the long journey. In fact, they openly criticized him again and again for not taking the right course. One day Columbus got tired of it, and since they were having breakfast, he took a boiled egg (a very unlikely item on a trans-Atlantic ship of that time) and asked his critics to balance the egg on its tip. They each took turns trying but did not succeed. Columbus let them fail, then grabbed the egg and smashed it on the table so that the broken shell was flat and the egg stood still. "Anybody could do that!" said one of the captains. "Sure you could, but you didn't think of it," said Columbus. "Now let me run my own ship."

There is a fine line between being authoritarian and being decisive, but you want to find that line and stop there. If you have perpetually disgruntled employees in your firm, you may want to consider getting rid of them no matter how valuable they are. People who spend all their time proving that you don't know what you are doing will never help you build a good firm and will poison the atmosphere for everybody else. Don't be held hostage by your own employees.

One of the most common problems that creates such an atmosphere of disgruntlement is the lack of accountability in the firm. If employees are not held accountable for the results they generate and are left unsupervised, this frequently results in a sense of dissatisfaction by those who are trying to contribute but find themselves constrained by the chaotic state of project management in the firm. Managing employees is nothing else but setting goals and making sure those goals are achieved.

Frequently advisors are afraid to tell employees that they are not doing a good job. In fact, most advisors are horrified to write performance evaluations and prefer to write anonymous evaluations rather than tell their employees what they are unhappy with something. Unfortunately, when you never criticize, your praise also loses value. In fact, it creates a sense that you don't care.

Leadership does not tolerate a vacuum. If you are not acting like a leader of your own firm, you will find that your employees will start challenging you or challenging each other for that leadership spot. This is not a positive result—it will only result in infighting and a toxic atmosphere. That's not to suggest that you should keep employees from leadership opportunities—on the contrary, this is important. At the end of the day, though, you have to make it clear that you are the leader of this firm. If you don't lead your own firm, somebody else will and you will not like it.

## Agree to Disagree—aka Avoiding Difficult Decisions

Eventually in every partnership you will come to decisions that are important and that you don't agree on. These may concern the performance of an employee, the compensation of a staff person, the pricing of a service, the strategy for approaching a referral source, or any of the hundreds of decisions you will make together. When that time comes you will have to find a way as partners to deal with that disagreement in a way where you take action but you don't burn the bridges between you. If you try to "agree to disagree" and simply not address the issue, it will sooner or later become a sore spot in your relationship and the ensuing conflict will be even more severe.

Unresolved issues will kill your decision making and will spill into every area of management. It is not uncommon for one partner to express their dissatisfaction with one issue by arguing on a completely unrelated matter. Doesn't that remind you of a marriage? For that reason, you want to confront and put issues to rest quickly and decisively.

The whole point of being a good partner is that at some point you will do something that you disagree with but you will do it nonetheless. Being a good partner is not expressed through doing what you wanted to do in the first place. It is expressed by doing something you don't want to do. In other words, you have to accept that on some issues you will have to take action you disagree with and that's okay.

If you are the majority owner of the firm, you can't use your voting power to reach a decision on divisive issues—you have to make an argument and try to convince your partners. If that fails, you have to let them win at times even if you disagree. It is my opinion that you cannot outvote your partner more than once or twice in your career as partners. Every next episode will lead to increased resentment and a sense among the minority partners that they have no control. That's why partners leave successful firms to start their own practice—to seek more control.

To resolve difficult management decisions, you can try to formalize the process. Preparing more formal arguments for the discussion will help a lot to reach a comfortable decision. Perhaps doing some analysis and research and preparing projections will help you make a better decision on hiring a new research analyst (random example). The formality and depth of your argument will be more convincing and will also steer the discussion away from this simply being "your opinion." It is also fair to ask your partners to prepare such more formal analysis (but only if you do the work too).

## The Porch of Indecision[1]

Every business changes over time. Some changes are dramatic and perhaps painful. However, even painful decisions have to be made, and the planning has to yield to action. Failing to act results in a firm that "withers on the vine." Such indecision is particularly damaging if one partner is eager to act while the other is stalling. The most common issues that arise are:

- Hiring an employee.
- Creating a succession plan.
- Changing partner compensation.
- Rebranding the firm.
- Developing a different approach to business development.
- Changing broker-dealers.

You can always ask your partner for more time to make a decision, but if that time is measured in years, you have to consider the possibility that the lack of action is a decision in itself.

## People Who Don't Develop

One of the most difficult aspects of trying to grow a firm is trying to accelerate the growth of your employees. The needs of the firm and the opportunities to take on responsibility usually run far ahead of the ability of the employee advisors to handle those responsibilities. Unfortunately, very often the advancement of an employee on his or her career path slows down or even stops completely. It is not uncommon for employee advisors to progress to the point of being able to service existing relationships and then never really progress to being able to develop new relationships.

Dealing with employees who are performing well in their current job but are not progressing is one of the most difficult and stressful decisions in running an ensemble. Unfortunately, when this happens it literally threatens to halt the growth of the entire firm, especially if the employee in question is the only employee advisor.

There is a very high level of expectation on the first one or two employee advisors in a firm. They need to grow fast and develop into lead advisors and future partners. If the first one or two advisors stall in their growth, they block the path for future growth of the firm. Since they are not growing past the service position the firm will have a hard time affording more salaries and the owner(s) need to personally generate the additional growth. What is more, it becomes likely that a more recent hire will catch up with the incumbents and even surpass them. When this occurs, some level of friction between the employees is very likely and inevitably that stress crosses over to the principals.

There is absolutely nothing wrong with employing career service people. A service advisor who never transitions to business development can still be very productive in the firm and enjoy a rewarding career. It just cannot be the first two or three employee advisors. A firm with five or more employee advisors can afford service specialists. A firm with two or three advisors cannot. There is simply not enough business development capacity to create a career for a pure service specialist.

The decision is very difficult, but unfortunately I would generally encourage my clients to hire another advisor who can grow faster and perhaps limit the compensation of the incumbent at the service position. Often this means pushing out a good and loyal employee, but the only alternative is a stagnating firm.

## Protecting Your Ensemble

Managing a firm is a job full of very difficult decisions and is often very stressful. Managing your own level of stress and never letting yourself succumb to the desire to just let your emotions run free is very difficult. Unfortunately, you will soon find that this is the only way to avoid the pitfalls of partnership conflicts and employee friction.

Partnerships can be very fragile. They require constant maintenance and support and they fracture easily. They are grounded in trust and respect, and both of those qualities are very difficult to develop but very easy to lose. A partnership requires work, and at time it may feel like too much work. Still, you have to always remember why you have a partner—because he or she will help you grow faster, protect you when things are tough, and share with you all their knowledge, energy, and heart—that's a lot!

## Note

1. The Porch of Indecision is a section of Jimmy Buffett's Margaritaville Orlando cafe that I came across and simply loved the name.

# CHAPTER 14

# Doing Deals

As I write this chapter, valuations of advisory firms are at an all-time high, and the pace of deals is accelerating. As you read this chapter, there may be acquisition frenzy in the industry or there may be rapidly declining interest in owning advisory firms and rapidly dropping values. Both are equally likely and all depend on the actions of consolidators. Consolidation drives a rush for the remaining targets and a quick spike in valuations. As soon as acquirers draw out of the market, the deals dry up and the remaining industry buyers become much more selective and careful in their acquisitions. Consolidators are extremely active now, and their activity is driving the market—their fate, however, is uncertain. As you are managing the equity of your ensemble firm, you need to always create internal options and internal liquidity to protect your firm from the vagaries of the consolidation-dependent mergers and acquisitions (M&A) world.

Witness the accounting industry—in the 1990 consolidators such as American Express and Century Business Systems were buying accounting firms throughout the country and had driven values to as high as two times their revenue. Today, following the demise of those efforts and the wave of mergers it precipitated, the valuations of accounting firms are down to 0.75 to 1.20 times the revenue of the firm. [1]

The general principles of buying and selling advisory markets have been thoroughly covered in Mark Tibergien's book, *How to Value, Buy or Sell an Advisory Practice*, as well as an excellent series of research reports by FPTransitions (www.fptransitions.com) and FA Insight (www.FAinsight. com). What I want to focus on in this chapter is the implementation of equity planning and internal deals specifically for ensembles. In addition, I want to share some of my experience working with firms that have gone through a sale to a consolidator or other type of acquirer.

## Equity Planning for Ensembles

As an ensemble firm, your equity is your reward for the risk and hard work. It is also a valuable resource that you have to carefully manage. This includes using the equity as a retention tool (Chapter 8 discusses introducing new partners) as well as thinking ahead and planning for the exit of the firm's partners. The external market is certainly a solution for exiting the business, but it usually implies substantial changes to the company—perhaps even the end of its existence. Internal equity transactions can provide an alternative to selling the firm. They may also end up being more reliable, less risky, and allowing more control of the terms of your exit.

### The Number of Partners Is Important

Before embarking on the exit from the business, you are likely to add a number of partners to your ensemble firm. Depending on how many individuals you see as your partners in the next 10 to 15 years, you will find that you can pursue different strategies for managing your equity.

Firms that anticipate a high number of partners (more than five or six) have the advantage of a broad pool of potential business leaders and are less dependent on one owner. On the other hand, such firms need to be very deliberate in planning for the exit of the first generation of partners, since the problem of retiring an entire generation of business owners may be insurmountable. In addition, with a high number of owners, you will need to establish management structures that are somewhat independent of ownership. Finally, you will need to consider the possibility that a partner will leave the firm, not as a retirement act but rather in order to join another firm or work on her or his own. These issues need to be considered carefully and planned for.

In firms where there is one large shareholder (founder) who holds the majority of the equity, equity planning should begin as soon as the firm reaches over $2 million in revenue, perhaps even earlier. The larger the firm grows, the more difficult it will be for the minority owners to buy out the majority owner. The earlier the firm starts preparing for that event, the better the chances for success are.

What happens in a lot of highly successful firms is that the equity holdings of the owner appreciate well beyond the financial means of the minority owners. Such firms end up with the founder holding $10 million or more in equity, and the combined financial resources of the junior partners are nowhere near sufficient to provide a buy-out. This essentially paints the firm in the corner in the sense that it can only sell to an external acquirer. Internal transition becomes unattainable.

If preparation starts early enough, there is no reason why an external acquisition should be the only option. First of all, in a highly successful firm (this problem only occurs in large and successful firms) the minority owners should theoretically be able to borrow against the equity of the firm to complete a purchase. Such a leveraged buyout is, after all, the original purpose for the existence of private equity firms. While many private equity firms have shifted toward working with public companies and billion-dollar IPO candidates, there still remain many who provide funding for buyouts.

Unlike a consolidation deal, buyouts allow the firm to repay its obligation to the private equity lender and recoup all of its shares and control. The cost of such funding is high and the process of obtaining approval is not an easy one. Then again, it can be argued that the most expensive form of funding is selling the firm.

In addition to leveraged buyout (LBO) strategies, some firms use a process of "serial redemption" where the majority owner starts early on a committed schedule of selling their shares to the minority shareholders or the company itself. The early start is critical in such cases. As the firm is growing, it is also appreciating. As the firm appreciates, it becomes more difficult to pass the equity to the next generation. Starting early and using small "doses" of equity, owners can get ahead of the appreciation and help the next generation assume control.

In all such strategies of yearly sale to the minority owners, there should be an understanding that this is not the best way to maximize the value of the equity. It is primarily a way of creating liquidity and "getting chips off the table." Naturally, in a growing firm, the majority owner will maximize their value by staying invested in the firm. However, that decision will come at the cost of being stuck with a highly valuable but also highly illiquid chunk of private company stock. Some liquidity may be preferable even if it leaves money on the table.

In many firms, there will be a generation of senior owners (founders) and a generation of younger partners. Such generational transfers can make the process easier since the firm is not heavily dependent on just one single owner, but at the same time this can create a real scheduling problem of who gets to leave the firm when. It is very important to avoid a "rush to the door" among the senior partners.

The only way to establish an orderly transition for an entire generation of founders is to recruit a large group of second-generation owners and for the founders to be very constructive and honest in their dialogue with each other. Both are necessary conditions and neither one is sufficient in itself. Ideally, the plans of the founders are not identical, and the firm can take some time to get to the desired end-state. Much like the orderly closing of a bank, though, no one is allowed to panic and try to rush out. If that happens, then the only possible outcome is the sale of the firm.

There is no need to become very technical and to engage investment bankers from day one in order to create an equity plan for your firm. All you need is depth of ownership and a mutual understanding of how the transition will occur. Most of all, the younger owners will need to understand what it will take to retire the founders without losing the firm. They need to be comfortable with the alternatives and willing to take some risk. No risk, no return, or as my father will put it (quoting the British marines), "no guts, no glory!"

I will never forget having a meeting with a large registered investment advisor (RIA) firm with a classic combination of two founders and six younger partners. One of the founders had already retired and the other founder was almost done buying him out (perhaps a mistake). The purpose of the meeting was to establish a process through which the remaining founder would retire in five to 10 years. The firm was worth well over $10 million at the time and quickly growing in value. The founder queried his partners whether they would be willing to take the risk of borrowing some capital to buy him out. The answer was "Yes, yes, of course!" Encouraged, the founder asked what would be the extent of the risk they would take. "Maybe $100,000 or $200,000 per partner," was the somewhat hesitant answer. I could see the horror in the founder's eyes. Needless to say, the sale of the firm was just a matter of time.

Internal transitions between owners are not somehow inherently superior. In fact, they take a long time to prepare, present a significant risk during that preparation, and tend to generate lower valuations. So why not just sell the firm? The answer lies in the terms and timing of the exit. Selling the firm usually means five to seven years of hard transition work and an increasingly difficult process of watching another entity take over your life's work. Transitioning internally can mean a process of slowing down, while still enjoying the work with clients and seeing the firm continue one's legacy. Of course, not every internal transition is smooth and not every sale is a hostile takeover. In fact, consolidation deals often offer the notion that both can be achieved. Can you really have your cake and eat it too?

## Consolidation Deals

Consolidators play an important and valuable role in the industry—they provide liquidity and offer alternatives for succession. Consolidators use different names and many don't like to be called consolidators, or least of all "roll ups." Most serial acquisition models essentially boil down to the same financial model and pattern of transition. Fundamentally, the consolidators pay a high valuation for a portion of the firm's equity, typically 30 percent to 60 percent (most prefer to remain minority owners) with the goal of at some point taking the collection of firms they have acquired public and thus realizing the "private to public" arbitrage in valuations. The equity interest of the consolidator is usually structured as preferred stock or preferred interest with some very strong rights on the cash flow of the firm and tight restrictions on the activities of the principals outside of the firm.

The consolidation financial structures differ from each other, and some achieve a level of complexity, but at the bottom of all the models, the consolidator values the firm based on its earnings before owner compensation (EBOC) and the ultimate price boils down to a multiple of that number. In every single case, the acquirer receives a preferred interest in the earnings of the firm, making sure that the future cash flows from the firm to the acquirer supersede anything and everything, including owner compensation. The concept is very effective and elegant—the discretionary element of owner compensation and spending is removed, and the remaining number can be drawn upon for dividend payments. What is more, it allows owner to get to a very high valuation by putting their compensation at risk.

### Beware the Minority Interest

The minority interest purchased by the consolidators can be a very heavy burden on a firm and essentially act as a "Trojan horse" reducing the value of any and all future transactions. The deal appears to be at very high valuation but it discounts the value of the remaining interest severely. The preferred position of the earnings paid to the consolidators and their legal rights combined generate this effect.

In all such deals, the buyer receives an essentially guaranteed dividend from the firm. For example, if ABC Financial acquired a 30 percent interest in Target Advisory Services (TAS), the deal is usually structured as ABC buying 100 percent of the equity of TAS but then signing a contract with a management company formed by the principals of TAS that allocates

70 percent profit interest to the new company (TAS management or TASm). However, and this is a big deal, the 30 percent interest of ABC is ahead of TASm in line for dividends AND the definition of profit excludes any compensation to owners.

For example, assume TAS has $1,500,000 in earnings before owner compensation (EBOC) and was valued at six times EBOC or $9 million—a fantastic value. In most consolidator structures, ABC is now due a preferred dividend of $450,000 (30 percent of the earnings acquired) every year. If the actual EBOC is higher than the base acquired of $1,500,000, then the actual 30 percent is paid; if the EBOC is lower, then at least $450,000 is paid.

Notice that the preferred dividend is BEFORE any compensation to the owners. Assume for a moment that we are in 2009 and that EBOC declined to $500,000 from its high of $1,500,000. This means that ABC still gets $450,000 and the principals of the firm have to live on $50,000 between them. The pain of declining profit is borne entirely by the principals, the gain is shared. This structure led many firms to essentially pay their acquirers in 2008 and 2009 and not earn any compensation at all. That's the reason I was saying that valuations are high because owners put their paycheck at risk together with their equity.

In addition to the preferred dividend, the consolidation structures tend to erode the value of the remaining shares in the company by restricting the number and type of buyers. Following a consolidation deal, the company is no longer available to external buyers; it can only be sold internally. Not that there is a contractual restriction on external buyers, but rather there is a logical one—no bank or other RIA will buy such a restricted and subordinated claim to the company's profits.

As a result of the "internal-only" market for the remaining equity of the firm, the valuations may end up being very low. The buyers here have a very strong position—they are the only buyers. The net result is that typically the residual interest in the management company gets passed at low or no value to the next generation. In fact, a low valuation may be the only way to create an upside in the stock for the next generation. At times, there are also transactions between firms within the same consolidator due to the absence of internal buyers.

Some of the companies that are active in this space look for creative ways to get around this issue by setting up a pool of capital available to the second generation of owners who are buying out the original partners in the company. This pool of capital can support the value of the residual shares, but the higher price may make it difficult for the next generation to get an equity return. We really don't have enough history to judge what happens at that stage.

## What Changes and What Doesn't

Much of the appeal of consolidation deals is in the proposition that "nothing will change." Owners believe that they will continue running their firm exactly as they have in the past with minimal if any interference from the acquirer. This expectation, however, is not very realistic.

The development of a consolidation company can be divided into two parts—(1) acquisition phase and (2) mature operation. In the acquisition phase, the company is focused on acquiring companies and doing deals is at the center of its activities. The phase can last from four or five years to six or seven. During this time, companies are acquired and largely left alone after the deal. They only convert to basic accounting, human resource, and legal infrastructure but are not asked to make any significant changes in their operation.

Eventually, when the company goes public it has to demonstrate to its shareholders that it can generate organic growth in earnings and revenue (also referred to as "same store sales"). This is when the stance on operations tends to change and it becomes more likely that the consolidator will seek to create synergies and promote streamlining of operations.

The standardization of operations is not necessarily a bad thing. The use of common custodians, common software platforms, and common broker-dealers can give clients favorable pricing and can improve the quality of resources in every practice. The company can also develop centralized resources that were simply not available before, such as research capabilities or customized portfolio solutions. Unfortunately, most of the time advisors find such changes to be very intrusive and have a hard time coming to terms with them.

Consolidator deals bring about high valuations and liquidity to the advisory industry. At the same time, before taking the consolidator deals, advisors have to be clear what they are getting into. They have to be realistic about the residual value remaining in the company as well as the preferred rights of the consolidator. Everything works out very well in companies that grow quickly following the deal. However, if the company stagnates or even suffers a decline in revenue, the deal tends to unravel in a painful way for all participants.

## Other Acquirers

Banks were the most active acquirers in 2005 and 2006, and before the financial crisis financial institutions led the demand for financial advisory firms. CPA firms also acquired several large registered investment advisory firms to serve as their wealth management subsidiaries. In all of the acquisitions, the advisory firm not only benefits from a good price and the solid balance sheet of the acquirer (in 2008 it turned out the banks were not as solid as we thought) but also from the synergy of the services. The large client base of a bank or CPA firm promises to provide advisors with tremendous opportunity for growth.

Unfortunately, following the crisis, banks largely disappeared as acquirers of advisory firms. Perhaps the issues related to cleaning their balance sheets and demonstrating stability were too distracting to continue down the acquisition route. What is more, there were cases such as the Boston Private acquisitions (Boston Private had acquired several large and prominent wealth management firms) where the firms acquired were sold back to their original owners.

The key to bank and CPA acquisitions was integration of services and management structure. The integration between banking and wealth management services holds tremendous appeal but rarely materializes in practice. Unfortunately, bankers often have little understanding of the financial planning and investment advice provided by the new subsidiary. Reciprocally, advisors tend to have little knowledge of the banking process and products and tend to view them with high level of suspicion. The distrust is found on both sides and is equally unfair.

The knowledge gap can perhaps be overcome if the firm integrates well within the overall organizational structure of the bank. However, that proves to be even more difficult. Advisors have spent their independent career in a small organization with less than 20 employees and have a very difficult time understanding how to work with a bank that has 20 different levels of vice presidents. To compound the problem, compensation in the advisory industry is dramatically different from that in banking and as a result, the advisors often have higher salary expectations than the bank president.

These skeptical paragraphs should not suggest that bank acquisitions are doomed or that advisors should never sell to a bank. Rather, I would like to emphasize that advisors who are considering a bank partner should spend a lot of time considering the integration issues.

Ultimately, it should also be clear that a bank acquisition will leave little room for a second generation of owners to be "owners." They will find engaging careers as bank executives but there will no longer be that direct ownership connection to the business. This, in fact, may not be such an issue—many second-generation leaders in advisory firms are not ready or do not want to be owners. CPA firms with their large partnership structure leave more opportunity for equity engagement, but it should be clear that partners in a large CPA firm have much less control than partners in a small advisory firm.

## Finding Your Deal

No matter what your exit plan is or how committed you are to a specific alternative, you will always do well if you develop broad ownership. The presence of multiple owners and the possibility of internal buyouts will create higher value as well as give you the ability to control the pace and timing of your exit.

It is prudent to remember that neither the liquidity nor the valuations in the current market are guaranteed to last. The value of a professional services business is always a somewhat fuzzy concept. That's why internal equity strategies are so important. Value is created by profitability and transferability. As long as you have a profitable ensemble firm with internal transferability, you can always rely on high valuation upon your exit.

## Note

1. P. Dermot O'Neill, "How to Value an Accounting Firm," *The National Accountant*, August 2003.

# CHAPTER 15

# The Future Belongs to Ensembles

The financial advisory industry is very young as far as industries go. It has only been in existence for the last 20 to 30 years, and the majority of firms that are in business today were started in the last 10 to 15 years. The youth of the industry means that it is not only full of promise and energy but also uncertainty. We are testing different business models and different organizational forms in order to find the ones that are the most competitive, most profitable, and offer the most sense of personal success and achievement to the owners. I firmly believe that when the dust settles, we will find that the most competitive and successful firms of the future will be the true ensemble firms.

Industries are shaped by competition from the outside and the "culture of the industry" from the inside. Especially in professional service industries, competition alone does not determine the outcome. It determines the prominent services and pricing, but the marketplace behavior of the competitors is always somewhat a function of their shared culture—accountants tend to compete in very reserved and introverted ways, consultants will be creative and dazzling, and doctors will be informative and somewhat above the marketplace. The same is true for the way firms organize themselves—some industries are inherently team oriented and collaborative while others tend to rely on mavericks and individuals. The past of the financial advisory industry is a very individualistic one, but its culture is changing rapidly and its future should be one of collaboration.

Ensembles are more profitable, grow faster, and have more value. We spent quite a bit of time explaining why and how, and we found that the capacity, leverage, and expanded talents of an ensemble firm create more competitive service models. What is more, the resources of a larger firm allow investment in marketing, business development, specialized services, and better technology. The biggest advantage of ensembles, though, comes from their ability to attract and retain better professionals

If there is only one significant change you can make to your business this year, you should consider adding another professional. There is no other change that can bring so many positive results—capacity, productivity, and leverage. It will also bring new energy, new skills, and a new talent to the firm. Of course it will have to be the right person, in the right position, and at the right time, but in a rapidly growing industry the firms that act quicker and more decisively tend to gain the advantage.

Most of all, I hope you realize by now that the process of creating an ensemble is the process of cultivating people and relationships. The same amount of patience and care that professionals reserve for their clients should go into growing the employee and partner relationships. Without the care and patience it will be difficult to obtain the result. People don't grow their skills and careers on their own—they need an example, support, and opportunities. There is no other tie to a firm that is as strong as having that firm create your career. The firm that grew your career will be very difficult to leave and will always get a special effort and energy out of you. Owners of advisory firms can use that process to create a lasting relationship with their employees and future partners.

If you are a solo practitioner and you are contemplating converting to an ensemble practice model, you will find that many other advisors are pondering the same decision. If you explore your professional network and your closest colleagues, you may find that there are great professionals who are looking to join forces with an advisor like you. The interest in mergers is higher than it has ever been. You will also find that there are many young, talented people looking to join our industry and eager to devote their energy to the career of being a financial advisor. In other words, your future partners and associates are out there—all you have to do is reach out.

If you are in the middle of transformation to an ensemble, you have likely already learned the value of patience and consistency. Rome was not built in a day and an ensemble is not built in a year, or two, or three. Along with the patient investment in people and structure you should already be seeing the return on that investment. You should already be enjoying a collegiate atmosphere, the higher quality of service that a team can deliver, and the relief of not being the only person who has to think of everything.

Ensemble firms are complicated—they involve many people with different preferences, personalities, and goals. The larger the firm, the more complex the decisions become including operations, finances, compensation, and business development. The only way to manage that complexity is to embrace it. As the firm grows, you will find that you spend more and more of your time managing the business . . . and that's a good thing. Growing an ensemble firm means becoming a CEO and thinking like one. The strategies in this book are not meant to be recipes; they are more ways of thinking than specific instructions. Much like playing a chess game, managing a firm is a constant process of developing and executing a strategy while looking for tactical opportunities and also making sure that you do not become the victim of tactical mistakes. In other words, you will have to constantly try to look a few moves ahead while not messing up the move right in front of you.

We went through many bullet point lists of steps toward building compensation processes, equity structures, and career paths. We discussed many numeric formulas and analytical constructions. However, I hope you realize by now that the ensemble practice is not so much a legal, equity, or business structure as it is a cultural phenomenon. There is no structure that guarantees that you and your partners will share clients, profits, and equity. Instead, the patient accumulation of experiences and examples will shape your relationship with your partners and your staff. In turn, your relationships with your partners and your staff will shape your firm. Choosing the right business models and structures is important, but even more important is setting the right example, building the right culture in the firm, and developing the right relationship with your partners. This culture can be summarized in three simple words—"share, trust, and respect."

The future belongs to ensembles. The combined resources, skills, and capacity of a good team will outperform the solo or silo advisor model. Most of all, the energy and drive of a team will be much better at sustaining the enthusiasm and involvement of the professionals and creating a balanced life for the owners. A business is a live organism—it grows and it flourishes but it can wither and suffer. It needs nourishment and space to grow. Businesses are nourished by people—their time, their energy, their talent. People need opportunity, encouragement, and resources to prosper. People need other people who can help them, who can guide them, and who can be their colleagues and friends. One person alone cannot sustain this cycle, but a team, an ensemble, can keep it growing and improving. Ensembles don't just create more profit and more equity; they create people—talent, energy, and effort. The people then create everything else.

If you have read this far, you have likely made up your mind long ago that you will follow the path to building an ensemble firm. I hope the thoughts in this book will give you some useful guidance, ideas, and practical methods to accelerate that process. Most of all, I hope you realize that an ensemble practice is a way of thinking and working in an environment of trust, respect, and collaboration. The future belongs to ensemble firms and ensemble firms belong to you—the business owners and professionals who join forces to build something bigger and better for the benefit of your clients, your employees and for your own career and legacy.

# About the Author

**PHILIP PALAVEEV** is an industry expert and consultant focused on improving the profitability and value of financial services firms. Philip is the owner and CEO of The Ensemble Practice LLC (www.ensemblepractice.com), a management consulting firm helping financial advisors build profitable and valuable partnerships. The firm works with a select group of advisors who are looking to create and grow an ensemble. Palaveev also works with broker-dealers and custodians on creating impactful practice management services for their advisors.

Philip has been the president of Fusion Advisor Network, a network of independent advisors that changed the way broker-dealers deliver business management and camaraderie to their clients. As president, Palaveev was responsible for the strategy of the firm and led its growth from a fast-growing start-up to one of the industry's most innovative and successful firms.

Until 2008, Palaveev was a principal in Moss Adams LLP, an accounting and consulting firm with industry-leading expertise in practice management. Philip led the market research for Moss Adams as well as consulted with hundreds of advisors and broker-dealers.

Philip Palaveev is also the author of multiple research papers and articles and is a frequent speaker at industry conferences. He lives in rainy Seattle, WA, with his wife and two children. Philip is also a reluctant marathon runner and an amateur boxer with more concussions than victories. He enjoys and welcomes all comments, questions, and e-mails.

# Index